加油！
jiā yóu
Chinese for the Global Community
Workbook 2

许嘉璐 主编
XU Jialu

陈绂　　王若江　　朱瑞平
CHEN Fu　WANG Ruojiang　ZHU Ruiping

娄毅　　杨丽姣　　李凌艳　　Pedro ACOSTA
LOU Yi　YANG Lijiao　LI Lingyan

Printed in China

中国国家汉办赠送
Donated by Hanban, China

CENGAGE Learning™

北京师范大学出版集团
BEIJING NORMAL UNIVERSITY PUBLISHING GROUP
北京师范大学出版社

加油!
jiā yóu

Chinese for the Global Community

Workbook 2 with Audio CDs

Publishing Director / CLT Product Director: Paul Tan
Product Manager (Outside Asia): Mei Yun Loh
Senior Development Editor: Lan Zhao
Associate Development Editor: Coco Koh
Product Manager (Asia): Joyce Tan
Country Manager (China): Caroline Ma
Account Manager (China): Arthur Sun
CLT Coordinator (China): Mana Wu
Assistant Publishing Manager: Pauline Lim

北京师范大学出版集团
BEIJING NORMAL UNIVERSITY PUBLISHING GROUP
北 京 师 范 大 学 出 版 社

Executive Editors: Fan Yang, Lili Yin
Graphic Designer: Baofen Li
Illustrator: Hai Bo
Proofreader: Han Li
Sound Engineers: Guangying Feng, Wei Wang, Shuai Wang
Sound Editor: Zhangji Wei

Cover and Layout Design: Redbean De Pte Ltd
Photos: Getty Images, unless otherwise stated

© 2008 Cengage Learning Asia Pte Ltd and
Beijing Normal University Press

Printed in Singapore
2 3 4 5 6 7 8 9 10 SL 12 11 10 09

ISBN: 978-981-4221-67-2 (International)
ISBN: 978-7-303-09024-2 (Mainland China)

For product information and orders, contact your local Cengage Learning or BNUP sales representatives. Or visit our Websites at
www.cengageasia.com or **www.bnup.com.cn**
For permission to use material from this text or product, email to
asia.publishing@cengage.com

Cengage Learning products are represented in Canada by Nelson Education, Ltd.

CENGAGE LEARNING

Asia Head Office (Singapore)
Cengage Learning Asia Pte Ltd
5 Shenton Way #01-01
UIC Building
Singapore 068808
Tel: (65) 6410 1200
Fax: (65) 6410 1208
Email: asia.info@cengage.com

United States
Heinle, Cengage Learning
20 Channel Center Street
Boston, MA 02210
Tel: (1) 800 354 9706
    (1) 617 757 7900
Fax: (1) 800 487 8488

China
Cengage Learning Asia Pte Ltd
(Beijing Rep Office)
Room 1201, South Tower, Building C
Raycom Info Tech Park
No. 2, Kexueyuan South Road
Haidian District, Beijing, China 100080
Tel: (86) 10 8286 2096
Fax: (86) 10 8286 2089
Email: asia.infochina@cengage.com

Beijing Normal University Press

China
No. 19 Xinjiekouwai Street
Beijing, China 100875
Tel: (86) 10 5880 2833
Fax: (86) 10 5880 6196
Email: yll@bnup.com.cn
       fan@bnup.com.cn

Author's Message

Jia You! Chinese for the Global Community is specially written for anyone who seeks to learn about the Chinese culture and people, and to use this knowledge in the context of the global community.

The most important aim of learning another language is to be able to exchange ideas with people of another culture. In order to achieve this, you need to learn about the culture of the people you wish to communicate with. From this perspective, a good textbook should contain rich cultural content. It should also provide the learner with a variety of exercises and reference materials so that they can get more practice in using the language.

It was in accordance with the above principles that we wrote this textbook series. It was created by a team of distinguished Chinese and American scholars who are experts in both Chinese language teaching, and subjects such as educational psychology, Chinese history, and culture.

If you already have some knowledge of Chinese and would like to go on learning, then this textbook series is definitely suitable for you. We hope it will inspire you to lifelong learning about the Chinese language and people.

We are keen to hear feedback from students and teachers who use this textbook series. This will be of great help to us, and will also help in strengthening friendship between the Chinese and American people.

Xu Jialu

PRINCIPAL
College of Chinese Language and Culture
Beijing Normal University, China

Preface

The Workbook exercises are thematically linked to the content of each lesson, allowing students to apply newly-acquired vocabulary, sentence patterns, and cultural knowledge to new and meaningful tasks. The Workbook is a useful tool for assessing the student's grasp of the materials learned in the program and for furthering their communication and language skills.

The Workbook exercises can be used as instructional activities, as homework, or as timed assessments. The Workbook activities cover all four skills (listening, reading, writing, and speaking), three communicative modes (interpretive, interpersonal, and presentational), as well as cultural knowledge.

The Workbook format and question types are designed to resemble the AP Chinese Language and Culture exam; students taking the AP Chinese exam can therefore get extensive practice on the exam format. The Workbook can also be used by any intermediate student of Chinese who is looking for additional comprehensive language practice.

The exercises in each lesson are divided into two sections. Section One, which consists of multiple-choice questions, assesses the student on listening and reading comprehension. Section Two, which consists of free-response questions, assesses students on oral and written communication.

- **Listening Comprehension (Multiple Choice)** – There are two categories of listening exercises.

    ▸ The first category of listening exercises assesses interpersonal communication skills by requiring the student to listen to recordings of short conversations and then identify the appropriate continuation of each from a list of possible answers.

    ▸ The second category of listening exercises requires the student to listen to recordings of short Chinese texts in the form of announcements, conversations, instructions, broadcasts, messages or reports, and then answer multiple-choice questions about them. Students are allowed to take notes. These exercises assess interpretative communication skills; the student has to comprehend different forms of spoken Chinese, and identify main ideas and supporting details.

- **Reading Comprehension (Multiple-Choice)** – These exercises assess interpretative communication skills by requiring the student to answer questions about different types of reading texts (letters, notices, notes, signs, e-mails, or stories).

- **Writing (Free Response)** – The four questions in this section assess communication skills in the interpersonal and presentational modes by requiring the student to write in four different styles.

  ▸ Story Narration – The student has to produce a written narrative of a story as depicted by a series of pictures.

  ▸ Personal Letter – The student has to write a response to a letter from a pen pal, describing personal experiences, expressing preferences, and justifying opinions.

  ▸ E-Mail Response – The student has to read an e-mail from a friend and produce an appropriate written response.

  ▸ Relay a Telephone Message – The student has to listen to a voice telephone message and then relay the message by typing a note to a friend or family member.

- **Speaking (Free Response)** – The three questions in this section assess oral communication skills in the interpersonal and presentational modes.

  ▸ Simulated Conversation – The student has to respond orally to a series of thematically linked questions as part of a simulated conversation.

  ▸ Cultural Presentation – The student has to make an oral presentation describing and explaining the significance of a Chinese cultural practice or product.

  ▸ Event Plan – The student has to make an oral presentation on a plan for an event such as a fundraising fair, a three-day holiday trip, or an outdoor class activity.

Answer sheets for Section One multiple choice questions are provided at the end of each lesson. The Workbook comes with 3 audio CDs. The CDs provide the audio program for all listening activities.

Contents

UNIT SIX
LESSON 11 Man and Nature
When a Tsunami Hits

Section One

I. Multiple Choice (Listen to the dialogs)

Note: In this part, you may NOT move back and forth among questions.

Directions: In this part, you will hear several short conversations or parts of conversations followed by four choices, designated (A), (B), (C), and (D). Choose the one that continues or completes the conversation in a logical and culturally appropriate manner. You will have 5 seconds to answer each question.

1.	(A)	(B)	(C)	(D)	5.	(A)	(B)	(C)	(D)
2.	(A)	(B)	(C)	(D)	6.	(A)	(B)	(C)	(D)
3.	(A)	(B)	(C)	(D)	7.	(A)	(B)	(C)	(D)
4.	(A)	(B)	(C)	(D)	8.	(A)	(B)	(C)	(D)

II. Multiple Choice (Listen to the selections)

Note: In this part, you may move back and forth only among the questions associated with the current listening selection.

Directions: In this part, you will listen to several selections in Chinese. For each selection, you will be told whether it will be played once or twice. You may take notes as you listen. After listening to each selection, you will see questions in English. For each question, choose the response that is best according to the selection. You will have 12 seconds to answer each question.

Selection 1

1. Which of the following animals does the woman think is the smartest?
   (A) Dog
   (B) Cat
   (C) Dolphin
   (D) Monkey

2. How does the man feel about the woman's pet?
   (A) He dislikes her pet.
   (B) He is curious about her pet.
   (C) He is very fond of her pet.
   (D) He does not think that her pet is special.

3. According to the conversation, which of the following statements is TRUE?
   (A) The man thinks his pet is too obedient.
   (B) The man rears a cat.
   (C) The woman is surprised at the talents of the man's pet.
   (D) The woman does not like cats.

Selection 2

4. What does Wang Nan think about Li Yan's absence?
   (A) She heard that Li Yan is sick.
   (B) She thinks that Li Yan may have forgotten about the class.
   (C) She guesses that Li Yan is away.
   (D) She is unsure about the reason for Li Yan's absence.

5. What topic was covered during the lesson?
   (A) The climate in West Asia
   (B) The climate in Southeast Asia
   (C) The impact of global warming on the Middle East
   (D) The impact of global warming on South Asia

6. What is Wang Nan's main purpose in calling Li Yan?
   (A) To tell Li Yan that there will be a test in the next lesson
   (B) To confirm the reason for Li Yan's absence
   (C) To tell Li Yan what happened during the lesson
   (D) To ask Li Yan if she would like to join her for a discussion

Selection 3

7. According to the weather forecast, what will the weather be like in the afternoon?
   (A) Cloudy
   (B) Sunny
   (C) Snowy
   (D) Rainy

8. What does the woman mean when she says "这个天气预报可真准(這個天氣預報可真準)"?

   (A) The weather forecast is accurate.

   (B) The swallows' behavior predicts the weather accurately.

   (C) The insects' behavior is a good indicator of the weather.

   (D) Man is able to make a more accurate forecast than animals.

9. According to the conversation, which of the following statements is TRUE?

   (A) In a sense, swallows can predict the weather.

   (B) It began raining just before the conversation started.

   (C) The woman thinks the man's arguments are nonsensical.

   (D) Before it rains, insects can be observed to fly higher than normal.

Selection 4

10. What is TRUE about the panda base?

    (A) It is located in the south of Sichuan.

    (B) It is the largest panda base in the world.

    (C) It has 200 pandas in total.

    (D) It is far away from Chengdu.

11. What does "寿星(壽星)" mean in the text?

    (A) The cutest panda   (B) The weakest panda

    (C) The oldest panda   (D) The most popular panda

12. Why was the panda given the name "川川(川川)"?

    (A) It was named after the place it lives.

    (B) It was found near a stream.

    (C) It likes the sound of water.

    (D) It was transported from Beijing to Chengdu.

Selection 5

13. What does the woman plan to do for summer?

    (A) Visit her friend in Phuket   (B) Travel with her family to Phuket

    (C) Learn photography in Phuket   (D) Take a field trip to Phuket

14. Why is the woman worried about her vacation plan?

    (A) The climate may affect her flight schedule.

    (B) The traveling cost may exceed her budget.

    (C) She is worried about the tsunami.

    (D) She may not enjoy the company of her traveling partner.

15. According to the conversation, which of the following statements is TRUE?

    (A) The woman is an expert in tsunami.

    (B) Waves triggered by a tsunami can reach over 20 meters in height.

    (C) The man suggests that the woman change her plan.

    (D) It is said that more tsunamis are expected over the next few years.

III. Multiple Choice (Reading)

Note: In this part, you may move back and forth among all the questions.

Directions: You will read several selections in Chinese. Each selection is accompanied by a number of questions in English. For each question, choose the response that is best according to the selection.

Read this e-mail.

[Simplified-character version]	[Traditional-character version]
发件人: 王佳 收件人: 高浩 主　题: 我在东北哈尔滨 日　期: 8月12日	發件人: 王佳 收件人: 高浩 主　題: 我在東北哈爾濱 日　期: 8月12日
小浩: 　　你好! 　　我昨天到了东北哈尔滨,这是个很美丽的现代化城市。我们住在一个很安静的宾馆里,离宾馆不远就是穿城而过的松花江。今天我们刚刚去了郊外的野生动物园,它和一般动物园不同的是,因为怕野生动物攻击游客,所以我们只能坐在中巴车里观赏动物,而动物们则在园内自由地活动。这个野生动物园正在试营业期间,里边的动物还不是很多,大致分为三个区,第一个是草食动物区,比如长颈鹿什么的,第二个是雉类园区,里边有山鸡、驼鸟之类的动物,第三个是猛兽区,不过这个区的动物还没进园,我想下次你来的时候,一定可以看到凶猛的大型动物了!我会继续给你写信,告诉你我的所见所闻。 　　　　　　　　　　　　　王佳	小浩: 　　你好! 　　我昨天到了東北哈爾濱,這是個很美麗的現代化城市。我們住在一個很安靜的賓館裏,離賓館不遠就是穿城而過的松花江。今天我們剛剛去了郊外的野生動物園,它和一般動物園不同的是,因爲怕野生動物攻擊遊客,所以我們只能坐在中巴車裏觀賞動物,而動物們則在園內自由地活動。這個野生動物園正在試營業期間,裏邊的動物還不是很多,大致分爲三個區,第一個是草食動物區,比如長頸鹿什麽的,第二個是雉類園區,裏邊有山鷄、駝鳥之類的動物,第三個是猛獸區,不過這個區的動物還沒進園,我想下次你來的時候,一定可以看到凶猛的大型動物了!我會繼續給你寫信,告訴你我的所見所聞。 　　　　　　　　　　　　　王佳

1. According to Wang Jia, how is Harbin like?
   (A) It is a beautiful ancient city.
   (B) There is a river flowing through the city.
   (C) There is a wildlife zoo in the city center.
   (D) It is a quiet small town.

2. What does "试营业（試營業）" refer to in the passage?
   (A) A small-scale enterprise
   (B) A business operation that is launched before the scheduled date
   (C) A trial business operation before the official opening
   (D) An examination that tests one's business knowledge

3. Which of the following statements about the wildlife zoo is TRUE?
   (A) It is located beside the Songhua River.
   (B) There have been cases where animals have attacked visitors.
   (C) There are ferocious animals in the zoo.
   (D) Visitors are allowed to tour around only by the zoo bus.

Read this weather forecast.

[Simplified-character version]

天气预报：
　　今天天气晴转阴。白天最高温度26℃，夜间最低温度20℃。北转南风2~3级。
　　今天白天晴转多云，风力不大，空气清新凉爽，有利于大家进行户外活动。

空气湿度预报：
　　今天白天本市最小相对湿度是30%，夜间最大相对湿度是60%。

紫外线指数预报：
　　今天紫外线气象指数是4，白天光照条件比较好，紫外线照射强度强，户外活动时注意防晒。

[Traditional-character version]

天氣預報：
　　今天天氣晴轉陰。白天最高溫度26℃，夜間最低溫度20℃。北轉南風2~3級。
　　今天白天晴轉多雲，風力不大，空氣清新涼爽，有利於大家進行戶外活動。

空氣濕度預報：
　　今天白天本市最小相對濕度是30%，夜間最大相對濕度是60%。

紫外線指數預報：
　　今天紫外線氣象指數是4，白天光照條件比較好，紫外線照射強度強，戶外活動時注意防曬。

4. Which of the following statements about the weather forecast is TRUE?

(A) People should bring along an umbrella if they are going outdoors.

(B) People should dress to keep themselves warm.

(C) Outdoors activities are not recommended.

(D) People should apply sunscreen if they are going for outdoor activities.

5. Which of the following statements describe the weather for that day?

(A) Mild temperature, dry and strong wind

(B) Mild temperature, mild wind, strong sunshine

(C) High temperature, strong wind, mild humidity

(D) Low temperature, mild wind, low humidity

6. According to the forecast, we can infer that "紫外线指数（紫外線指數）" is related to
_____ .

(A) humidity in the air

(B) level of air pollution

(C) amount of sunlight

(D) intensity of the wind

Read this passage.

[Simplified-character version]	[Traditional-character version]
罗布泊位于中国西部，是一片没有人烟的荒漠，自然条件非常恶劣。1900年，瑞典人斯文·赫定 (Sven Hedin) 带领探险队穿越罗布泊进行考古工作。一天，因为要寻找探险队里唯一的铁锹，本地向导奥尔得克暂时离开了队伍，直到第二天他返回队伍时赫定才得知：昨晚后半夜起大风，奥尔得克迷了路，无意间闯入一个遗址，发现那儿到处散落着木雕和木材，于是特意带回一块精美的木雕做样品。赫定发现那是一两千年之前的装饰木板，并推断用它来装饰的建筑一定不是普通人家的房屋。实际上，那天晚上奥尔得克发现的地方就是史书记载中消失了一千六百年的古代城市——楼兰。这一发现后来被称为是20世纪最重要的百大考古发现之一。	羅布泊位於中國西部，是一片沒有人煙的荒漠，自然條件非常惡劣。1900年，瑞典人斯文·赫定 (Sven Hedin) 帶領探險隊穿越羅布泊進行考古工作。一天，因爲要尋找探險隊裏唯一的鐵鍬，本地向導奧爾得克暫時離開了隊伍，直到第二天他返回隊伍時赫定才得知：昨晚後半夜起大風，奧爾得克迷了路，無意間闖入一個遺址，發現那兒到處散落著木雕和木材，於是特意帶回一塊精美的木雕做樣品。赫定發現那是一兩千年之前的裝飾木板，並推斷用它來裝飾的建築一定不是普通人家的房屋。實際上，那天晚上奧爾得克發現的地方就是史書記載中消失了一千六百年的古代城市——樓蘭。這一發現後來被稱爲是20世紀最重要的百大考古發現之一。

7. Why did Sven Hedin lead his men across Lop Nur?

(A) They wanted to conquer the harsh natural conditions.

(B) They wanted to challenge their own limits.

(C) They wanted to carry out archaeological work.

(D) They wanted to find the ancient city of Loulan.

8. Why did the local guide insist on looking for the shovel?

(A) It was precious.

(B) It was an artifact.

(C) He wanted to return it to the owner.

(D) It was the only shovel in their possession.

9. What was the ruins the local guide found by chance that night?

(A) An ancient city recorded in the annals

(B) A place that produced wood and wood products

(C) A mansion occupied by nobles in ancient times

(D) A city that specializes in woodcarvings

Read this passage.

[Simplified-character version]	[Traditional-character version]
江苏大丰的麋鹿自然保护区里生活着134头麋鹿。麋鹿是鹿科的一种，它的长相奇特，角似鹿非鹿，脸似马非马，蹄似牛非牛，尾似驴非驴，因此又称"四不像"。几个月前，自然保护区的工作人员在野外考察时发现了一只受伤的小麋鹿，于是把它带回工作站进行救治。经过精心呵护，小麋鹿已经完全康复。一个星期前，工作人员依依不舍地把小麋鹿放回了野外，并在过去的一个星期中对它进行了跟踪观察。可是他们发现小麋鹿并没有完全适应野外的环境。不知道如何觅食和寻找水源，而且也不愿意接近其他麋鹿。专家认为，这是因为人工喂养了一段时间后，小麋鹿的生活习性有了一定的改变，所以短时间还不能完全适应野生的环境，他们将继续对小麋鹿进行追踪观察。	江蘇大豐的麋鹿自然保護區裏生活著134頭麋鹿。麋鹿是鹿科的一種，牠的長相奇特，角似鹿非鹿，臉似馬非馬，蹄似牛非牛，尾似驢非驢，因此又稱"四不像"。幾個月前，自然保護區的工作人員在野外考察時發現了一隻受傷的小麋鹿，於是把牠帶回工作站進行救治。經過精心呵護，小麋鹿已經完全康復。一個星期前，工作人員依依不捨地把小麋鹿放回了野外，並在過去的一個星期中對牠進行了跟蹤觀察。可是他們發現小麋鹿並沒有完全適應野外的環境。不知道如何覓食和尋找水源，而且也不願意接近其他麋鹿。專家認爲，這是因爲人工餵養了一段時間後，小麋鹿的生活習性有了一定的改變，所以短時間還不能完全適應野生的環境，他們將繼續對小麋鹿進行追蹤觀察。

10. Which of the following statements about the Père David's Deer is TRUE?

   (A) They can only be found in China's Jiangsu province.

   (B) They are not a species of deer.

   (C) They share physical traits with four different animals.

   (D) They are not easily tamed.

11. What is the association between the calf and the workstation?

   (A) It was discovered at the vicinity of the workstation.

   (B) It was wounded in the vicinity of the workstation.

   (C) It was unwilling to leave the workstation.

   (D) It was brought back to the workstation by someone.

12. What observation about the calf was made after it left the workstation?

   (A) Its injury could not heal completely.

   (B) It had become dependent on human feeding.

   (C) It was attacked by its own species.

   (D) It adapted well to its natural habitat.

Read this passage.

[Simplified-character version]	[Traditional-character version]
有一架小型飞机中途发生故障，驾驶员在一条州际公路上降落。这里车辆稀少，只看见不远处开来一辆车，驾驶员跳出机舱向这辆车走过去，希望能搭便车到最近的出口。这辆汽车缓缓地停在路旁，坐在驾驶座的女人探出头紧张地说："我会马上走开的，先生，只要您告诉我怎么回到公路上，我会把车子尽快开离飞机场的。"	有一架小型飛機中途發生故障，駕駛員在一條州際公路上降落。這裏車輛稀少，只看見不遠處開來一輛車，駕駛員跳出機艙向這輛車走過去，希望能搭便車到最近的出口。這輛汽車緩緩地停在路旁，坐在駕駛座的女人探出頭緊張地説："我會馬上走開的，先生，只要您告訴我怎麼回到公路上，我會把車子儘快開離飛機場的。"

13. This account is most likely a _____ .

    (A) myth

    (B) joke

    (C) news item

    (D) fable

14. Why did the pilot walk up to the car?

    (A) He wanted to ask for directions.

    (B) He wanted to tell the woman to leave quickly.

    (C) He wanted the woman to give him a lift.

    (D) He wanted to help the woman.

15. Why was the woman nervous?

    (A) She thought she had encountered a criminal.

    (B) She thought she had missed her flight.

    (C) She feared that the man would want a lift.

    (D) She thought she had committed an offence.

Read this information.

[Simplified-character version]	[Traditional-character version]
名　　称: 金丝猴 　　　　（中国特有的猴类） 体貌特征: 体长53~77厘米，尾巴与体 　　　　长差不多；毛厚而长，毛色 　　　　鲜艳；脸呈淡蓝色，嘴唇 　　　　宽厚，鼻子向上翘，因而又 　　　　名"仰鼻猴"。 习性: 　　　多栖息于海拔2000~3000米的深 山中，夏季在海拔高的山林中活动， 冬季下到较低地区。喜欢群居，有十几 只一群的，也有上百只一群的，成群游 荡，有一定的活动范围和相对固定的 路线。 食性: 　　　以野果、树叶、嫩枝芽为主，也吃 苔藓植物。	名　　稱: 金絲猴 　　　　（中國特有的猴類） 體貌特徵: 體長53~77厘米，尾巴與體 　　　　長差不多；毛厚而長，毛色 　　　　鮮豔；臉呈淡藍色，嘴唇 　　　　寬厚，鼻子向上翹，因而又 　　　　名"仰鼻猴"。 習性: 　　　多棲息於海拔2000~3000米的深 山中，夏季在海拔高的山林中活動， 冬季下到較低地區。喜歡群居，有十幾 隻一群的，也有上百隻一群的，成群遊 蕩，有一定的活動範圍和相對固定的 路線。 食性: 　　　以野果、樹葉、嫩枝芽爲主，也吃 苔藓植物。

16. The information above is most likely _____ .

   (A) an explanation of an animal's characteristics

   (B) a paper on animal research issues

   (C) a record of animal sightings

   (D) a classification of animals

17. Which of the following is a physical characteristic of the golden monkey?

   (A) It has thin lips and blue eyes.

   (B) It has a dark blue face.

   (C) Its tail is as long as its body.

   (D) Its fur is short but thick.

18. According to the passage, which of the following statements about the golden monkey is TRUE?

   (A) The Snub-nosed monkey is one of their species.

   (B) It does not like to live alone.

   (C) It is only active in low-lying lands.

   (D) Its diet consists of only fruits and insects.

Read this passage.

[Simplified-character version]

菲律宾气象局指出，由于全球持续变暖，菲律宾低洼地区及岛屿被不断上升的海水吞噬，国土面积正逐渐缩小。菲律宾气象局官员胡安尼洛在一次讲演中说，从1961年到2003年，菲律宾群岛周围的海平面每年以1.8厘米的速度上升。有"千岛之国"美誉的菲律宾，在海水落潮时可以看见7108座岛屿，而涨潮时其中一座已完全消失，还有五千多座则面积明显缩小。如果海平面继续上升，不用10年的时间，将会有更多岛屿被淹没。胡安尼洛认为海平面上升的原因是全球变暖，南北极冰山融化。她呼吁世界各国减少二氧化碳的排放，防止温室效应加剧。

[Traditional-character version]

菲律賓氣象局指出，由於全球持續變暖，菲律賓低窪地區及島嶼被不斷上升的海水吞噬，國土面積正逐漸縮小。菲律賓氣象局官員胡安尼洛在一次講演中說，從1961年到2003年，菲律賓群島周圍的海平面每年以1.8厘米的速度上升。有"千島之國"美譽的菲律賓，在海水落潮時可以看見7108座島嶼，而漲潮時其中一座已完全消失，還有五千多座則面積明顯縮小。如果海平面繼續上升，不用10年的時間，將會有更多島嶼被淹沒。胡安尼洛認爲海平面上升的原因是全球變暖，南北極冰山融化。她呼籲世界各國減少二氧化碳的排放，防止温室效應加劇。

19. Which of the following numbers is closest to the increased sea surface height around Philippines from 1961 to 2000?

(A) 60 centimeters

(B) 70 centimeters

(C) 75 centimeters

(D) 80 centimeters

20. How is the greenhouse effect affecting the Philippines?

(A) Many animal species are facing extinction.

(B) Half of its islands have disappeared completely.

(C) The average yearly temperature has been fluctuating.

(D) Many islands have become smaller.

21. Where would this information most likely come from?

(A) A government notice

(B) A personality profile

(C) A news report

(D) A weather forecast

Read this public sign.

[Simplified-character version]

咨询台

[Traditional-character version]

諮詢臺

22. Where would this sign most likely appear?

(A) In an office

(B) At a railway station

(C) At a bus stop

(D) In a gym

23. What kind of information can you most likely get here?

(A) Transport information

(B) Weather forecast

(C) Information about matches

(D) Latest news reports

Read this public sign.

[Simplified-character version]

限高4米

[Traditional-character version]

限高4米

24. Where would this sign most likely appear?

　(A)　On one side of a bridge

　(B)　At a road junction

　(C)　Inside a building

　(D)　At the entrance of a gym

25. What does this sign mean?

　(A)　Anything less than 4 meters is not allowed.

　(B)　Everything there is exactly 4 meters.

　(C)　Anything over 4 meters is not allowed.

　(D)　Everything there is higher than 4 meters.

Section Two

I. Free Response (Writing)

Note: In this part, you may NOT move back and forth among questions.

Directions: You will be asked to write in Chinese in a variety of ways. In each case, you will be asked to write for a specific purpose and to a specific person. You should write in as complete and as culturally appropriate a manner as possible, taking into account the purpose and the person described.

1. Story Narration

The four pictures present a story. Imagine you are writing the story to a friend. Narrate a complete story as suggested by the pictures. Give your story a beginning, a middle, and an end.

2. Personal Letter

Imagine you received a letter from a pen pal in Beijing. In the letter, he raises the issue of national forest resources. Write a reply in letter format. Share with him your thoughts and suggestions about the protection of national forest resources.

3. E-Mail Response

Read this e-mail from a friend and then type a response.

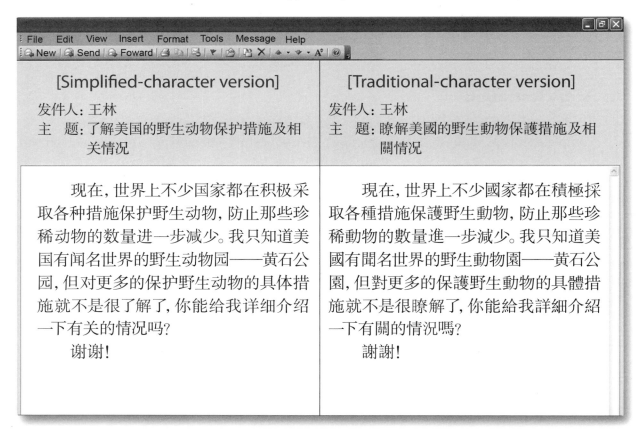

File   Edit   View   Insert   Format   Tools   Message   Help

New | Send | Foward

[Simplified-character version]

发件人：王林
主　题：了解美国的野生动物保护措施及相
　　　　关情况

　　现在，世界上不少国家都在积极采取各种措施保护野生动物，防止那些珍稀动物的数量进一步减少。我只知道美国有闻名世界的野生动物园——黄石公园，但对更多的保护野生动物的具体措施就不是很了解了，你能给我详细介绍一下有关的情况吗？

　　谢谢！

[Traditional-character version]

发件人：王林
主　题：瞭解美國的野生動物保護措施及相
　　　　關情況

　　現在，世界上不少國家都在積極採取各種措施保護野生動物，防止那些珍稀動物的數量進一步減少。我只知道美國有聞名世界的野生動物園——黄石公園，但對更多的保護野生動物的具體措施就不是很瞭解了，你能給我詳細介紹一下有關的情況嗎？

　　謝謝！

4. Relay a Telephone Message

Imagine your mother has gone on a business trip. You and your sister were not at home when she left. She calls you after arriving at her destination. You will listen twice to the message. Then relay the message, including the important details, by typing an e-mail to your sister.

II. Free Response (Speaking)

Note: In this part, you may NOT move back and forth among questions.

Directions: You will participate in a simulated conversation. Each time it is your turn to speak, you will have 20 seconds to record. You should respond as fully and as appropriately as possible.

1. Conversation

Imagine you are traveling to China. You are sitting in a taxi stuck in a traffic jam. You have a conversation with the taxi driver.

Directions: You will be asked to speak in Chinese on different topics in the following two questions. In each case, imagine you are making an oral presentation to your class or your family in Chinese. First, you will read and hear the topic for your presentation. You will have 4 minutes to prepare your presentation. Then you will have 2 minutes to record your presentation. Your presentation should be as complete as possible.

2. Cultural Presentation

Using the Qinghai-Tibet Railway in China as an example, share your understanding of man and nature coexisting in harmony. In your presentation, you should state clearly your understanding and ideas about the example and the issue.

3. Event Plan

Your school is organizing a safety exercise and you have been asked to plan it. In your presentation, explain your plan in detail, stating clearly the theme you wish to emphasize, the structure of the exercise, preparatory work needed, and the strengths and advantages of your plan.

UNIT SIX
LESSON 12 Man and Nature
Where Will We Live Tomorrow?

Section One

I. Multiple Choice (Listen to the dialogs)

Note: In this part, you may NOT move back and forth among questions.

Directions: In this part, you will hear several short conversations or parts of conversations followed by four choices, designated (A), (B), (C), and (D). Choose the one that continues or completes the conversation in a logical and culturally appropriate manner. You will have 5 seconds to answer each question.

1.	(A)	(B)	(C)	(D)	5.	(A)	(B)	(C)	(D)
2.	(A)	(B)	(C)	(D)	6.	(A)	(B)	(C)	(D)
3.	(A)	(B)	(C)	(D)	7.	(A)	(B)	(C)	(D)
4.	(A)	(B)	(C)	(D)	8.	(A)	(B)	(C)	(D)

II. Multiple Choice (Listen to the selections)

Note: In this part, you may move back and forth only among the questions associated with the current listening selection.

Directions: In this part, you will listen to several selections in Chinese. For each selection, you will be told whether it will be played once or twice. You may take notes as you listen. After listening to each selection, you will see questions in English. For each question, choose the response that is best according to the selection. You will have 12 seconds to answer each question.

Selection 1

1. What does the father think about rearing pets?
   (A) Their neighbors do not like pets.
   (B) Pets may be noisy and may disturb others.
   (C) The girl's mother does not like rearing pets.
   (D) Rearing pets is not an interesting activity.

2. According to the conversation, what do the father and the girl decide to do?

   (A) They will decide if they should rear pets later.

   (B) They will rear a dog immediately.

   (C) They will find out how to take good care of pets.

   (D) They will contact the girl's mother at once.

Selection 2

3. Which of the following can we infer from this selection?

   (A) The peony is the national flower of China.

   (B) The chrysanthemum flower is least mentioned in ancient poems.

   (C) The chinese orchid is one of the famous traditional flowers in China.

   (D) The blossoming period for the plum blossom lasts for 3-5 days.

4. Which of the following statements about the peony is TRUE?

   (A) It is very expensive.

   (B) It blooms for a week or two.

   (C) It is a big, fragrant flower.

   (D) Its petals are usually white.

5. When will the peony most likely blossom?

   (A) Late winter   (B) Late autumn

   (C) Late summer   (D) Late spring

6. According to the selection, what does the peony symbolize?

   (A) Love   (B) Auspiciousness

   (C) Wisdom   (D) Beauty

Selection 3

7. What did the woman plan to do initially?

   (A) Watch a movie on television

   (B) Read a book at home

   (C) Go out with friends

   (D) Surf the Internet at home

8. What kind of movie does the man want to watch?

   (A) A documentary

   (B) A comedy

   (C) A science fiction film

   (D) A musical

9. Why does the woman agree to go watch the movie at last?
   (A) She is interested in the movie.
   (B) The Internet service is down suddenly.
   (C) The man had already bought the tickets.
   (D) She does not want to stay at home alone.

Selection 4

10. Why does the speaker consider herself lucky?
    (A) It was not raining when she visited the zoo.
    (B) It is rare to see bamboos bloom.
    (C) She has discovered a new bamboo forest.
    (D) She was selected to take a photo with the pandas.

11. How often is the bamboo said to bloom?
    (A) Twice every 8 years   (B) Twice every 10 years
    (C) Once every 30 years   (D) Once every 60 years

12. According to the message, which of the following statements is TRUE?
    (A) Pandas do not like to eat bamboos in bloom.
    (B) Bamboos in bloom will affect the food sources for pandas.
    (C) Bamboos in bloom are poisonous.
    (D) Bamboos will wither away few years after they bloom.

Selection 5

13. When is the conversation most likely taking place?
    (A) In winter   (B) In autumn
    (C) In summer   (D) In spring

14. Why do the students decide to go to Zhongshan Park?
    (A) There are many activities there.
    (B) It is beautiful there.
    (C) It is near the city center.
    (D) They can go hiking there.

15. According to the conversation, which of the following statements is TRUE?
    (A) The students will probably not be in China in autumn.
    (B) The students are planning an overseas trip in spring.
    (C) The man's favorite season is summer.
    (D) The woman has never been to Zhongshan Park.

III. Multiple Choice (Reading)

Note: In this part, you may move back and forth among all the questions.

Directions: You will read several selections in Chinese. Each selection is accompanied by a number of questions in English. For each question, choose the response that is best according to the selection.

Read this passage.

[Simplified-character version]	[Traditional-character version]
冬虫夏草是一种很奇怪的东西。有人说到了冬天,它是动物,夏天来了,它又成了植物。这到底是怎么回事呢?原来在西藏、青海等地的高山草原上,每年夏秋季节,有几种飞蛾的幼虫会钻到地下找东西吃,并一直呆到冬天结束。有的幼虫把一种植物的种子吃进肚子,于是种子就在虫肚子里生长。种子"吃"着虫子体内的营养,一个冬天下来,就只剩下幼虫的外壳——这就是冬虫。到了第二年夏天,种子从幼虫的外壳里长出像小草一样的东西,这就是夏草。冬虫夏草能治很多病,身体不好的人吃了还可以增强体质,是一种名贵的药材。	冬蟲夏草是一種很奇怪的東西。有人說到了冬天,它是動物,夏天來了,它又成了植物。這到底是怎麼回事呢?原來在西藏、青海等地的高山草原上,每年夏秋季節,有幾種飛蛾的幼蟲會鑽到地下找東西吃,並一直呆到冬天結束。有的幼蟲把一種植物的種子吃進肚子,於是種子就在蟲肚子裏生長。種子"吃"著蟲子體內的營養,一個冬天下來,就只剩下幼蟲的外殼——這就是冬蟲。到了第二年夏天,種子從幼蟲的外殼裏長出像小草一樣的東西,這就是夏草。冬蟲夏草能治很多病,身體不好的人吃了還可以增強體質,是一種名貴的藥材。

1. Where may cordyceps be found?
   (A) In a desert
   (B) On a plateau
   (C) In a lake
   (D) In a rainforest

2. What kind of larvae may become cordyceps?
   (A) Those that crawl on the ground
   (B) Those that fly in the air
   (C) Those that live on plateaus and feed on animals
   (D) Those that live underground and feed on plants

3. How long does it take cordyceps to form?

   (A) About one month

   (B) About half a year

   (C) About one year

   (D) About one and a half years

Read this story.

[Simplified-character version]

从前有一位老人，整天坐在家里没有什么事情，久而久之就觉得浑身都不舒服。有一天，他睡在床上竟起不来了。家人给他请来了一个大夫，大夫仔细询问老人的情况以后，对老人说："你只要每天亲自上山去找一种草药，闻一闻就可以了。记住，一定要在山上闻，否则不会有效果。"说完，大夫就走了。老人照办了，果然没过多久，他的病全好了。老人的孙子特意去感谢那个大夫，"你不用谢我，要谢就谢那座大山吧！"医生解释说，"可是如果只让你爷爷去爬山，他肯定不会去的。所以……"

[Traditional-character version]

從前有一位老人，整天坐在家裏沒有什麼事情，久而久之就覺得渾身都不舒服。有一天，他睡在床上竟起不來了。家人給他請來了一個大夫，大夫仔細詢問老人的情況以後，對老人説："你只要每天親自上山去找一種草藥，聞一聞就可以了。記住，一定要在山上聞，否則不會有效果。"説完，大夫就走了。老人照辦了，果然沒過多久，他的病全好了。老人的孫子特意去感謝那個大夫，"你不用謝我，要謝就謝那座大山吧！"醫生解釋説，"可是如果只讓你爺爺去爬山，他肯定不會去的。所以……"

4. Why did the doctor ask the old man to climb the mountain to find herbs?

   (A) The doctor needed someone to help him collect herbs.

   (B) The herbs on the mountain smell good.

   (C) Only the herbs on the mountain can cure the old man's illness.

   (D) The old man needed to climb the mountain.

5. What did the grandson do after the old man recovered?

   (A) He made a special trip to thank the doctor.

   (B) He went to give thanks to the mountain.

   (C) He went to thank the doctor when he passed by his house.

   (D) He went to thank the doctor after he came back from the market.

6. What does the doctor attribute the old man's illness to?

(A) Old age

(B) Poor diet

(C) Too much sleep

(D) Lack of exercise

Read this passage.

[Simplified-character version]	[Traditional-character version]
乌鲁木齐——吐鲁番一日游 （单程，200公里）	**烏魯木齊——吐魯番一日遊** （單程，200公里）

特色：

乌鲁木齐——吐鲁番一日游

火焰山和葡萄沟是吐鲁番的名胜。火焰山以炎热闻名天下，看过《西游记》的朋友一定还记得，传说中它是孙悟空引来的天火烧成的，所以奇热无比。葡萄沟位于火焰山西侧的一个峡谷中，那里溪流环绕，布满了葡萄架，是一个清凉世界。游客沿途经过闻名于世的火焰山，再到葡萄架下用午餐，在一热一凉中感受吐鲁番。

行程：

清晨乘车前往吐鲁番葡萄沟。途中可以观赏火焰山、万佛宫、高昌故城。午餐后游葡萄沟，参观坎儿井，傍晚乘车返回乌鲁木齐。

费用：

500元。包含景点门票、空调车费、餐费和旅行社责任险。

注意：

新疆部分地区海拔较高，紫外线照射强烈，所以旅游者应准备充足、有效的防晒品。

报名电话：0991–3225555
联系人：张建新

特色：

火焰山和葡萄溝是吐魯番的名勝。火焰山以炎熱聞名天下，看過《西遊記》的朋友一定還記得，傳說中它是孫悟空引來的天火燒成的，所以奇熱無比。葡萄溝位於火焰山西側的一個峽谷中，那裏溪流環繞，佈滿了葡萄架，是一個清涼世界。遊客沿途經過聞名於世的火焰山，再到葡萄架下用午餐，在一熱一涼中感受吐魯番。

行程：

清晨乘車前往吐魯番葡萄溝。途中可以觀賞火焰山、萬佛宮、高昌故城。午餐後遊葡萄溝，參觀坎兒井，傍晚乘車返回烏魯木齊。

費用：

500元。包含景點門票、空調車費、餐費和旅行社責任險。

注意：

新疆部分地區海拔較高，紫外線照射強烈，所以旅遊者應準備充足、有效的防曬品。

報名電話：0991–3225555
聯繫人：張建新

7. What does "一热一凉（一熱一涼）" mean?

(A) The Flaming Mountain is hot, but travelers will feel cool after eating grapes.

(B) Urumchi is extremely hot, but Turpan is a cool city.

(C) Urumchi is hot when there is no wind and cool when wind blows.

(D) The Flaming Mountain is hot, but Grape Valley is cool.

8. What can travelers expect when they depart from Urumchi?

(A) Pass some scenic spots along the way

(B) Cross the Flaming Mountain

(C) Travel non-stop until they reach Turpan

(D) Stay the night at Turpan

9. According to the passage, which of the following statements is TRUE?

(A) The fee includes tips for the tour guide.

(B) Travelers are advised to bring sunscreen.

(C) Travelers are expected to buy their own travel insurance.

(D) The tour starts after lunch.

Read this passage.

[Simplified-character version]	[Traditional-character version]
汉长安城遗址距离西安市只有5公里。在西汉200多年间，这个城市一直是中国的政治、经济和文化中心。长安城历经三个时期才得以建成，公元前202年汉高祖刘邦开始修建皇宫，公元前194年汉惠帝开始修筑长安城，直到公元前104年长安城才全部建成。城内布局整齐，道路宽平，12辆马车可以并列行驶，道路旁栽种了松树和柏树，绿树成荫。全城共有8条大街，160个巷里，9个市区，最盛时城内人口近30万，是中国历史上第一个大城市。	漢長安城遺址距離西安市只有5公里。在西漢200多年間，這個城市一直是中國的政治、經濟和文化中心。長安城歷經三個時期才得以建成，公元前202年漢高祖劉邦開始修建皇宮，公元前194年漢惠帝開始修築長安城，直到公元前104年長安城才全部建成。城內佈局整齊，道路寬平，12輛馬車可以並列行駛，道路旁栽種了松樹和柏樹，綠樹成蔭。全城共有8條大街，160個巷里，9個市區，最盛時城內人口近30萬，是中國歷史上第一個大城市。

10. What is the passage mainly about?

(A) The history of Han Chang'an

(B) The time when Han Chang'an was built and its scale

(C) The modes of transportation in Han Chang'an

(D) The city layout of Han Chang'an

11. According to the passage, when was Han Chang'an completed?

   (A) In about A.D. 200

   (B) In about 200 B.C.

   (C) In about A.D. 100

   (D) In about 100 B.C.

12. According to the passage, which of the following statements is TRUE?

   (A) The streets of Chang'an are broad and neatly arranged.

   (B) Chang'an has been China's center of politics, economy, and culture since it was built.

   (C) Chang'an is far away from Xi'an.

   (D) The population in Chang'an has always been small.

Read this diary.

[Simplified-character version]

2007年4月2日　　星期一　　晴
　　今天从一个中国朋友那里听到一句话，"不到东北不知道胆有多小，不到广东不知道钱有多少"。这句话的意思是说住在东北的中国人勇敢豪爽，胆子大，而住在广东的人精明能干，懂经营会赚钱。确实如此，到中国以后，我发现中国很大，不同地区的人性格也不一样。江苏、浙江一带的人温和，而山东人呢，比较传统，因为那里是孔子的故乡。不同地区的人生活习惯也有很大差异，四川人爱吃辣的，山西人爱吃酸的，东北人爱吃咸的，南方人喜欢甜的。

[Traditional-character version]

2007年4月2日　　星期一　　晴
　　今天從一個中國朋友那裏聽到一句話，"不到東北不知道膽有多小，不到廣東不知道錢有多少"。這句話的意思是說住在東北的中國人勇敢豪爽，膽子大，而住在廣東的人精明能幹，懂經營會賺錢。確實如此，到中國以後，我發現中國很大，不同地區的人性格也不一樣。江蘇、浙江一帶的人溫和，而山東人呢，比較傳統，因爲那裏是孔子的故鄉。不同地區的人生活習慣也有很大差異，四川人愛吃辣的，山西人愛吃酸的，東北人愛吃鹹的，南方人喜歡甜的。

13. People from _____ are more traditional in nature.

   (A) Northeast China

   (B) Guangdong

   (C) Shandong

   (D) Shanxi

14. What are the characteristics of people from Guangdong?

    (A) Brave and outspoken

    (B) Astute and good at making money

    (C) Enterprising and timid

    (D) Mild and traditional

15. What does "不到东北不知道胆有多小（不到東北不知道膽有多小）" mean?

    (A) People in Northeast China are brave and forthright.

    (B) People in Northeast China are simple and plain.

    (C) People in Northeast China are timid.

    (D) People in Northeast China are very capable.

16. People from _____ like to eat spicy food.

    (A) Northeast China

    (B) Guangdong

    (C) Sichuan

    (D) Shanxi

Read this passage.

[Simplified-character version]	[Traditional-character version]
中国探险家陈亮法为实现自己的梦想，从1994年开始，一直用脚步丈量着中国的土地，已经历经了四十六难。1983年，16岁的陈亮法受《徐霞客游记》的影响，突然有了探险的想法，这一想法伴随了他好几年。直到1994年，他瞒着父母走上了探险的征途。接受采访时，他告诉我们，徒步探险最大的困难就是饥饿和孤独。有时候在茫茫大沙漠里，半个月都见不到一个人，但不管遇到怎样的困难，他都会坚持走下去。	中國探險家陳亮法爲實現自己的夢想，從1994年開始，一直用腳步丈量著中國的土地，已經歷經了四十六難。1983年，16歲的陳亮法受《徐霞客遊記》的影響，突然有了探險的想法，這一想法伴隨了他好幾年。直到1994年，他瞞著父母走上了探險的徵途。接受採訪時，他告訴我們，徒步探險最大的困難就是饑餓和孤獨。有時候在茫茫大沙漠裏，半個月都見不到一個人，但不管遇到怎樣的困難，他都會堅持走下去。

17. What prompted Chen Liangfa to start on his exploration?

    (A) He enjoyed investigating unknown regions.

    (B) He was influenced by a book.

    (C) His parents encouraged him to do so.

    (D) He dreamt about exploring new lands and decided to realize his dream.

18. According to the passage, which of the following statements about Chen Liangfa is TRUE?

   (A) He thought the greatest difficulties in his exploration were hunger and loneliness.

   (B) He began his exploration when he was 16 years old.

   (C) He is a member of the national exploration team.

   (D) He rode a bicycle wherever he went.

Read this passage.

[Simplified-character version]	[Traditional-character version]
苍鹭是一种能捕鱼的鸟,它在捕鱼时显示了惊人的技巧。它能把翅膀竖在头顶上,并伸开成伞的形状。伸开的翅膀在水面上产生了一个阴影,这个阴影能防止水面发生反射,这样,苍鹭便能清楚地看见水中的猎物,并在这个阴影内捉鱼。	蒼鷺是一種能捕魚的鳥,牠在捕魚時顯示了驚人的技巧。牠能把翅膀豎在頭頂上,並伸開成傘的形狀。伸開的翅膀在水面上產生了一個陰影,這個陰影能防止水面發生反射,這樣,蒼鷺便能清楚地看見水中的獵物,並在這個陰影內捉魚。

19. According to the passage, why do gray herons sometimes put their wings on their heads?

   (A) When they want to catch fish

   (B) When they want to escape from enemies

   (C) When they want to look at a distant object

   (D) When they want to attract mates

20. What enables gray herons to see fish in the water clearly?

   (A) They are very sensitive to fish's movements and can locate them easily.

   (B) They can fly close to the water surface.

   (C) They have good eyesight.

   (D) Their open wings can prevent reflection from the water.

21. What does "这个阴影（這個陰影）" refer to?

   (A) The open wings that are umbrella-shaped

   (B) The water surface with round ripples

   (C) The water surface with a shadow cast on it

   (D) A round pool

Read this public sign.

[Simplified-character version]

安全出口

[Traditional-character version]

安全出口

22. Where would this sign most likely appear?
   (A) At a scenic spot
   (B) In a theater
   (C) In a sports field
   (D) In a parking lot

23. What does this sign refer to?
   (A) An exit
   (B) An entrance
   (C) A backdoor
   (D) A side gate

Read this public sign.

[Simplified-character version]

无烟区

[Traditional-character version]

無煙區

24. Where would this sign most likely appear?
   (A) In an air-conditioned office
   (B) In a coffee shop
   (C) In a garden
   (D) At a playground

25. What does this sign mean?
   (A) This place is free from pollution.
   (B) This place is free from smoke and dust.
   (C) Discharge of fumes is forbidden here.
   (D) Smoking is forbidden here.

Section Two

I. Free Response (Writing)

Note: In this part, you may NOT move back and forth among questions.

Directions: You will be asked to write in Chinese in a variety of ways. In each case, you will be asked to write for a specific purpose and to a specific person. You should write in as complete and as culturally appropriate a manner as possible, taking into account the purpose and the person described.

1. Story Narration

The four pictures present a story. Imagine you are writing the story to a friend. Narrate a complete story as suggested by the pictures. Give your story a beginning, a middle, and an end.

2. Personal Letter

Imagine you received a letter from a pen pal in Beijing. The letter talks about the different living conditions in various Chinese cities, towns, and villages. Write a reply in letter format. Tell your pen pal what you think about the living conditions in different cities in the east and west coasts of the United States.

3. E-Mail Response

Read this e-mail from a friend and then type a response.

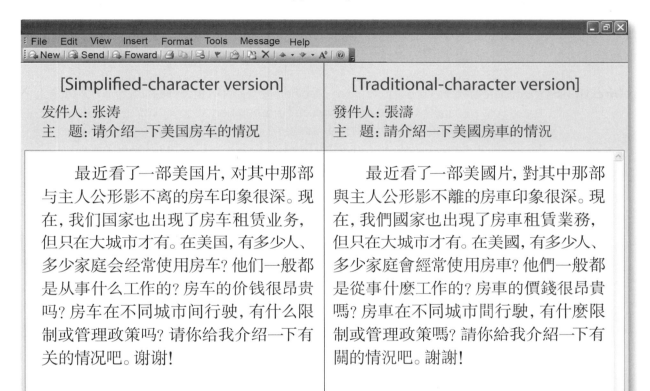

[Simplified-character version]	[Traditional-character version]
发件人: 张涛 主　题: 请介绍一下美国房车的情况	發件人: 張濤 主　題: 請介紹一下美國房車的情況
最近看了一部美国片, 对其中那部与主人公形影不离的房车印象很深。现在, 我们国家也出现了房车租赁业务, 但只在大城市才有。在美国, 有多少人、多少家庭会经常使用房车? 他们一般都是从事什么工作的? 房车的价钱很昂贵吗? 房车在不同城市间行驶, 有什么限制或管理政策吗? 请你给我介绍一下有关的情况吧。谢谢!	最近看了一部美國片, 對其中那部與主人公形影不離的房車印象很深。現在, 我們國家也出現了房車租賃業務, 但只在大城市才有。在美國, 有多少人、多少家庭會經常使用房車? 他們一般都是從事什麼工作的? 房車的價錢很昂貴嗎? 房車在不同城市間行駛, 有什麼限制或管理政策嗎? 請你給我介紹一下有關的情況吧。謝謝!

4. Relay a Telephone Message

Your brother's friend has made a call to him. You will listen twice to the voice message. Then relay the message, including the important details, by typing an e-mail to your brother.

II. Free Response (Speaking)

Note: In this part, you may NOT move back and forth among questions.

Directions: You will participate in a simulated conversation. Each time it is your turn to speak, you will have 20 seconds to record. You should respond as fully and as appropriately as possible.

1. Conversation

Imagine you are shopping in a departmental store in China. A salesgirl in the clothing department starts a conversation with you.

Directions: You will be asked to speak in Chinese on different topics in the following two questions. In each case, imagine you are making an oral presentation to your class or your family in Chinese. First, you will read and hear the topic for your presentation. You will have 4 minutes to prepare your presentation. Then you will have 2 minutes to record your presentation. Your presentation should be as complete as possible.

2. Cultural Presentation

Choose ONE rare animal in China. In your presentation, talk about your knowledge of the rare animal, including its basic characteristics, present living conditions, etc.

3. Event Plan

You and your partner are planning to organize an activity publicizing the need for environmental protection. In your presentation, tell your partner what you plan to do for this activity. Explain clearly the focus you wish to have, the main content you wish to publicize, the format of the event, etc. Also explain your tentative plan for the preparatory work required.

People and Society
The Hospitable Southwest

Section One

I. Multiple Choice (Listen to the dialogs)

Note: In this part, you may NOT move back and forth among questions.

Directions: In this part, you will hear several short conversations or parts of conversations followed by four choices, designated (A), (B), (C), and (D). Choose the one that continues or completes the conversation in a logical and culturally appropriate manner. You will have 5 seconds to answer each question.

1.	(A)	(B)	(C)	(D)		5.	(A)	(B)	(C)	(D)
2.	(A)	(B)	(C)	(D)		6.	(A)	(B)	(C)	(D)
3.	(A)	(B)	(C)	(D)		7.	(A)	(B)	(C)	(D)
4.	(A)	(B)	(C)	(D)		8.	(A)	(B)	(C)	(D)

II. Multiple Choice (Listen to the selections)

Note: In this part, you may move back and forth only among the questions associated with the current listening selection.

Directions: In this part, you will listen to several selections in Chinese. For each selection, you will be told whether it will be played once or twice. You may take notes as you listen. After listening to each selection, you will see questions in English. For each question, choose the response that is best according to the selection. You will have 12 seconds to answer each question.

Selection 1

1. Under what circumstances was this short speech most likely made?
    (A) During a family reunion
    (B) During a new year party
    (C) During a discussion
    (D) During a wedding

2. What is the most probable relationship between the speaker and Wang Cheng?

    (A) Father-in-law and son-in-law

    (B) Father and daughter

    (C) Husband and wife

    (D) Father and son

3. What does "他们的生活将展开新的一页（他們的生活將展開新的一頁）" mean?

    (A) It suggests that they are going to read a new book.

    (B) It signifies that they are going to start a new life overseas.

    (C) It means that their lives will undergo changes.

    (D) It is a congratulatory expression.

Selection 2

4. Why did the school arrange for the speaker to live with a Chinese family?

    (A) So that he can master the Chinese language easily and quickly

    (B) Because he did not want to stay in the foreign students' hostel

    (C) So that he can have the opportunity to have a better understanding of the Chinese way of life

    (D) Because there were no more rooms available in the foreign students' hostel

5. Where do the parents of his Chinese host family work?

    (A) In a college

    (B) In a high school

    (C) In an elementary school

    (D) In a company

6. How does the speaker get along with his Chinese host family?

    (A) He is nervous in their company.

    (B) He is very happy with them.

    (C) He is indifferent to them.

    (D) He is very close to them.

Selection 3

7. Who is the man looking for?

    (A) A woman with short hair

    (B) A woman who is a little dark

    (C) A woman who is rather short

    (D) A woman who has big eyes

8. According to the conversation, which of the following statements is TRUE?

    (A) The man saw the woman talk to Wang Lu in the gym.

    (B) The man was wearing a red shirt the day before.

    (C) The woman needs the man's help.

    (D) The woman is in the same class as Wang Lu.

Selection 4

9. Who is the woman in the conversation?

    (A) A student from the city of Wuhan

    (B) A student from one of the ethnic minorities

    (C) A reporter for the school newspaper

    (D) A teacher at the school

10. Why is the woman eating the food which she brought from home?

    (A) She has gastric problems.

    (B) She is a vegetarian.

    (C) The school cafeteria does not provide breakfast.

    (D) The breakfast provided by the school cafeteria does not cater to her needs.

11. Which of the following statements about the woman's breakfast situation is TRUE?

    (A) The school cafeteria will resolve the issue.

    (B) There is no solution to the situation.

    (C) The woman's boyfriend will come up with an alternative.

    (D) The school newspaper will help her solve the problem.

Selection 5

12. What is the woman's highest score for the electronic game?

    (A) Over 200,000

    (B) Over 100,000

    (C) Over 70,000

    (D) Over 30,000

13. Which of the following statements about how the man plays electronic games is TRUE?

    (A) He is a better player than the woman.

    (B) He is the top player in the class.

    (C) The woman is a better player than the man.

    (D) The man has just begun to learn how to play electronic games.

14. What is the relationship between the two speakers?

(A) Father and daughter

(B) Teacher and student

(C) Brother and sister

(D) Classmates

15. Why has the woman decided to stop playing electronic games for the time being?

(A) She has other interests now.

(B) The examination is just around the corner.

(C) She has been doing poorly in her studies.

(D) The school has banned the playing of electronic games.

III. Multiple Choice (Reading)

Note: In this part, you may move back and forth among all the questions.

Directions: You will read several selections in Chinese. Each selection is accompanied by a number of questions in English. For each question, choose the response that is best according to the selection.

Read this passage.

[Simplified-character version]	[Traditional-character version]
蒙古族人非常好客。进了蒙古包，不论认识还是不认识，客人坐下来就可以吃喝。据说有人骑马在草原上漫游，身上只背了一只羊腿，到了一户人家，就把这只羊腿解下来，客人吃喝一晚。第二天上路时，主人又给客人带上一只新鲜羊腿背着。回家时，这个人依然带着一只羊腿。蒙古人很实在，家里有什么，都拿出来招待客人。客人吃饱喝足，主人才高兴。这种风俗的形成，和长期的游牧生活有关。一家子住在大草原上，天苍苍，野茫茫，见到的牛羊比人多，他们很盼望远方的客人坐下来聊一聊。	蒙古族人非常好客。進了蒙古包，不論認識還是不認識，客人坐下來就可以吃喝。據說有人騎馬在草原上漫遊，身上只背了一只羊腿，到了一戶人家，就把這只羊腿解下來，客人吃喝一晚。第二天上路時，主人又給客人帶上一只新鮮羊腿背著。回家時，這個人依然帶著一只羊腿。蒙古人很實在，家裏有什麼，都拿出來招待客人。客人吃飽喝足，主人才高興。這種風俗的形成，和長期的游牧生活有關。一家子住在大草原上，天蒼蒼，野茫茫，見到的牛羊比人多，他們很盼望遠方的客人坐下來聊一聊。

1. Which of the following statements about the leg of lamb that the visitor brought home is TRUE?

   (A) It was purchased from the shepherds.

   (B) It was taken from his home and then brought back.

   (C) It was brought by him for someone else.

   (D) It was given as a gift by the shepherd in whose house he was a guest.

2. According to the passage, what are some of the characteristics of Mongols?

   (A) Smart, kind-hearted and hospitable

   (B) Honest, hospitable and generous

   (C) Determined, optimistic and passionate

   (D) Hospitable, honest and determined

3. Which of the following can we infer from the passage?

   (A) Visitors to a yurt must bring along a lamb.

   (B) Communication between nomadic Mongols and the outside world is scarce.

   (C) The way Mongols treat visitors is related to the climate.

   (D) The dietary habits of Mongols have been changing.

Read this passage.

[Simplified-character version]	[Traditional-character version]
维吾尔族人喜欢给别人取外号，几乎每个维吾尔男子都有外号。外号一般是朋友或者熟人根据一个人的性格或相貌特点来取的。另外，一个人的职业、身份、为人、爱好也会成为别人取外号的根据。维吾尔人的外号五花八门，许多外号可以当面叫，对方并不会生气。比如：一位外号叫"老牛"的人，路上碰见外号叫"西瓜"的邻居往家走，便问："伙计，您没买个西瓜带回来？""西瓜"回答："唉，我倒是买了一个西瓜，谁知今天有头老牛在市场上乱跑，一头冲过来把我的瓜撞坏了。"说完两人哈哈大笑，互相告别。	維吾爾族人喜歡給別人取外號，幾乎每個維吾爾男子都有外號。外號一般是朋友或者熟人根據一個人的性格或相貌特點來取的。另外，一個人的職業、身份、爲人、愛好也會成爲別人取外號的根據。維吾爾人的外號五花八門，許多外號可以當面叫，對方並不會生氣。比如：一位外號叫"老牛"的人，路上碰見外號叫"西瓜"的鄰居往家走，便問："伙計，您沒買個西瓜帶回來？""西瓜"回答："唉，我倒是買了一個西瓜，誰知今天有頭老牛在市場上亂跑，一頭衝過來把我的瓜撞壞了。"說完兩人哈哈大笑，互相告別。

4. What does "外号（外號）" mean?

(A) A nickname

(B) A family name

(C) The initials of a person's full name

(D) A formal title given to men

5. Which of the following statements about the Uighur people's "外号（外號）" is TRUE?

(A) It cannot be used in front of the elderly.

(B) It has rich origins.

(C) It is given when one becomes an adult.

(D) It must match their occupation.

6. Which of the following about the "old cow crashed into a watermelon" story in the passage is TRUE?

(A) It shows that the speaker is unhappy with his neighbor.

(B) It is a true story that just happened.

(C) It is just a joke.

(D) It is a myth.

Read this passage.

[Simplified-character version]	[Traditional-character version]
传说很早以前，北方草原上有个爱唱歌的蒙古族牧人，名叫苏和。他有一匹心爱的白马，白马的叫声非常动人。后来他失去了这匹白马，非常伤心。一次，在睡梦中，苏和看见白马嘶叫着向他跑来，就在这时他醒了。为了寄托对白马的怀念，苏和做出了草原上的第一支马头琴。琴杆的上端做成了马头的形状，演奏起来，声音柔和而深沉。从此，马头琴悠扬的琴声便和蒙古族这个爱马民族的草原生活联系在一起。	傳說很早以前，北方草原上有個愛唱歌的蒙古族牧人，名叫蘇和。他有一匹心愛的白馬，白馬的叫聲非常動人。後來他失去了這匹白馬，非常傷心。一次，在睡夢中，蘇和看見白馬嘶叫著向他跑來，就在這時他醒了。爲了寄托對白馬的懷念，蘇和做出了草原上的第一支馬頭琴。琴桿的上端做成了馬頭的形狀，演奏起來，聲音柔和而深沉。從此，馬頭琴悠揚的琴聲便和蒙古族這個愛馬民族的草原生活聯繫在一起。

7. Why did Su He create the musical instrument?

(A) He wanted to invent a new musical instrument.

(B) He wanted to get his white horse back.

(C) He wanted to remember his white horse.

(D) He wanted to sing the praises of the Mongolian grasslands.

8. According to the passage, what is the unique characteristic of the instrument?

    (A) It sounds like the neighing of a horse.

    (B) It produce sounds that are loud and sharp.

    (C) The body of the instrument is shaped like a horse.

    (D) The head of the instrument takes the shape of a horse's head.

9. What title would be most apt for the passage?

    (A) The Legend of the White Horse

    (B) The Legend of the *Matouqin*

    (C) The Musical Talents of Mongols

    (D) The Life of Su He

Read this passage.

[Simplified-character version]	[Traditional-character version]
北京的四合院很有名。为什么叫四合院呢？它们都是由四面建筑相合而成的一组建筑，所以叫四合院。以前北京人典型的家庭住房就是这样。一般是老人住北房，又称上房，完全向阳，冬暖夏凉；儿孙住东房、西房，又称东、西厢房；南房则用来接待客人或作其他用途。北京的胡同里几乎都是四合院。有的四合院院中套院，形成四合院群，以供大家族聚居，恭王府就是个典型。这种建筑形式反映了中国人重视家庭和睦的观念，以及与父母、子女、兄弟、姐妹共同生活的习惯。	北京的四合院很有名。爲什麼叫四合院呢？它們都是由四面建築相合而成的一組建築，所以叫四合院。以前北京人典型的家庭住房就是這樣。一般是老人住北房，又稱上房，完全向陽，冬暖夏涼；兒孫住東房、西房，又稱東、西廂房；南房則用來接待客人或作其他用途。北京的胡同裏幾乎都是四合院。有的四合院院中套院，形成四合院群，以供大家族聚居，恭王府就是個典型。這種建築形式反映了中國人重視家庭和睦的觀念，以及與父母、子女、兄弟、姐妹共同生活的習慣。

10. What is a "四合院（四合院）"?

    (A) A courtyard with four rooms

    (B) A courtyard surrounded by four houses

    (C) A type of building unique to Northern China

    (D) A type of building unique to Southern China

11. Why is the room in the north usually occupied by the elderly?

    (A) It is large.

    (B) It is quiet.

    (C) It is more comfortable.

    (D) It is easily accessible.

12. According to the passage, which of the following statements about the "四合院（四合院）" is TRUE?

    (A) Visitors usually stay in the house in the west.

    (B) Sons and grandsons live in the house in the south.

    (C) It reflects the Chinese notion of a harmonious family life.

    (D) It reflects the Chinese notion of hospitality.

Read this story.

[Simplified-character version]	[Traditional-character version]
有一天，一个小孩儿遇到一位神仙，他请求神仙带他去看"天堂"和"地狱"。于是神仙就把小孩儿带到一个大客厅里。客厅里的餐桌上摆满了丰盛的晚餐，一帮饿汉跑了进来，他们很想享用美食，可是客厅的主人告诉他们必须用筷子进食。这时他们才发现这里的筷子都是三尺长的。那么长的筷子，谁也无法将食物送到自己的嘴里。他们一筹莫展，只能继续挨饿。神仙说："孩子，你看，这就是地狱。"神仙又带孩子走到了另一个客厅，还是同样的晚餐，同样是三尺长的筷子，同样有一帮饿汉。但是这里的饿汉很聪明，他们两两合作，每个人都给对方夹食物，于是他们每个人都大吃了一顿。神仙意味深长地告诉孩子："这就是天堂。"	有一天，一個小孩兒遇到一位神仙，他請求神仙帶他去看"天堂"和"地獄"。於是神仙就把小孩兒帶到一個大客廳裏。客廳裏的餐桌上擺滿了豐盛的晚餐，一幫餓漢跑了進來，他們很想享用美食，可是客廳的主人告訴他們必須用筷子進食。這時他們才發現這裏的筷子都是三尺長的。那麼長的筷子，誰也無法將食物送到自己的嘴裏。他們一籌莫展，只能繼續挨餓。神仙說："孩子，你看，這就是地獄。"神仙又帶孩子走到了另一個客廳，還是同樣的晚餐，同樣是三尺長的筷子，同樣有一幫餓漢。但是這裏的餓漢很聰明，他們兩兩合作，每個人都給對方夾食物，於是他們每個人都大吃了一頓。神仙意味深長地告訴孩子："這就是天堂。"

13. Why is the first living room said to be hell?

    (A) People there cannot reach the food.

    (B) Everyone is gorging on the food.

    (C) There is nothing to eat.

    (D) People there are lazy.

14. How did the hungry people in the second living room manage to eat their fill?

(A) There were all kinds of food on the table.

(B) People there used the utensils ingeniously.

(C) The deities helped the people in that room.

(D) The utensils in that room were more suitable.

15. What does the story illustrate?

(A) Everyone should learn the proper way to use chopsticks.

(B) Everyone wishes to live in paradise, not in hell.

(C) Only people who can fill their stomachs are considered clever.

(D) People can live a happy life only by helping and loving each other.

Read this passage.

[Simplified-character version]	[Traditional-character version]
前些年, 中国人参加活动、聚会时, 见面第一句话往往是："您是哪个单位的？"而今, 却变成了："您在哪儿发财？"这反映出近年来人们思想发生的变化。	前些年, 中國人參加活動、聚會時, 見面第一句話往往是："您是哪個單位的？"而今, 卻變成了："您在哪兒發財？"這反映出近年來人們思想發生的變化。
以前, 人们习惯于求职打工, 以固定的工作机构、固定的工资为荣。现在随着市场经济的发展, 人们热衷于自己创业当老板, 做自己喜欢的事, 寻找适合自己发展的新天地, 这已经渐渐成了社会风气。人的社会化是中国改革的重要成果, 也是中国社会发展进步的一个重要标志。它意味着个人更加自由, 社会结构更加合理。	以前, 人們習慣於求職打工, 以固定的工作機構、固定的工資爲榮。現在隨著市場經濟的發展, 人們熱衷於自己創業當老板, 做自己喜歡的事, 尋找適合自己發展的新天地, 這已經漸漸成了社會風氣。人的社會化是中國改革的重要成果, 也是中國社會發展進步的一個重要標誌。它意味著個人更加自由, 社會結構更加合理。

16. What does "您在哪儿发财（您在哪兒發財）" mean?

(A) Asking where someone starts a business

(B) Asking where someone is working

(C) Asking where someone is living

(D) Asking where someone has made so much money

17. According to the passage, which of the following statements is TRUE?

(A) People like to earn a fixed salary now.

(B) People like to run their own businesses now.

(C) Pursuing higher salaries has become a trend in modern society.

(D) Pursuing societal change has become a trend in modern society.

Read this passage.

[Simplified-character version]	[Traditional-character version]
相传，在远古时代，黄帝和炎帝是居住在黄河地区的两个大部落的首领。那时候，人们抵抗自然灾害的能力很差，一遇到自然灾害就得搬家。有一次，炎帝部落被迫搬到黄帝部落居住的地方，他们觉得那儿条件很好，就决定长期住下去。黄帝部落的人起初并不愿意，于是双方就打起仗来。经过三次战斗，炎帝部落被打败了。炎帝表示愿意听从黄帝的命令，黄帝也同意让炎帝部落住下来。黄帝让人把造车、造船的技术教给炎帝部落的人，黄帝的妻子还亲自教他们如何养蚕抽丝。炎帝也把木犁和草药送给了黄帝。他们和睦相处，中华民族的历史由此揭开。中国人把黄帝和炎帝尊为中华民族的始祖，并自称为"炎黄子孙"。	相傳，在遠古時代，黃帝和炎帝是居住在黃河地區的兩個大部落的首領。那時候，人們抵抗自然災害的能力很差，一遇到自然災害就得搬家。有一次，炎帝部落被迫搬到黃帝部落居住的地方，他們覺得那兒條件很好，就決定長期住下去。黃帝部落的人起初並不願意，於是雙方就打起仗來。經過三次戰鬥，炎帝部落被打敗了。炎帝表示願意聽從黃帝的命令，黃帝也同意讓炎帝部落住下來。黃帝讓人把造車、造船的技術教給炎帝部落的人，黃帝的妻子還親自教他們如何養蠶抽絲。炎帝也把木犁和草藥送給了黃帝。他們和睦相處，中華民族的歷史由此揭開。中國人把黃帝和炎帝尊爲中華民族的始祖，並自稱爲"炎黃子孫"。

18. According to the passage, who were Huang Di and Yan Di?

    (A) They were two leaders of the same tribe.

    (B) They were relatives.

    (C) They were feuding enemies.

    (D) They were the forefathers of the Chinese people.

19. What can we infer about why Yan Di's tribe moved?

    (A) They liked to relocate.

    (B) They met with natural disasters.

    (C) They fancied the area where Huang Di's tribe lived.

    (D) They received an invitation from Huang Di's tribe.

20. According to the passage, why did Huang Di agree to Yan Di's request?

    (A) Huang Di was defeated.

    (B) Huang Di's wife persuaded him to agree to it.

    (C) Yan Di was willing to obey Huang Di's command.

    (D) Yan Di persuaded Huang Di to agree to it.

21. What skills did Yan Di's tribe acquire?

(A) Rearing silkworms, shipbuilding, carriage building, house building

(B) Rearing silkworms, silk reeling, using the wooden plow, collecting medicinal herbs

(C) Rearing silkworms, silk reeling, shipbuilding, carriage building

(D) Shipbuilding, carriage building, using the wooden plow, collecting medicinal herbs

Read this public sign.

[Simplified-character version]

谢绝参观

[Traditional-character version]

謝絕參觀

22. Where would this sign most likely appear?

(A) In a cafeteria

(B) In an airport lounge

(C) On a train

(D) At a television studio

23. What is the purpose of this sign?

(A) To thank visitors for their visit

(B) To welcome visitors

(C) To request that visitors do not enter

(D) To encourage visitors to make themselves at home

Read this public sign.

[Simplified-character version]

谁知盘中餐, 粒粒皆辛苦。

[Traditional-character version]

誰知盤中餐, 粒粒皆辛苦。

24. Where would this sign most likely appear?

(A) In a cafeteria

(B) In a hospital

(C) At a store

(D) At an information counter

25. What is the purpose of this sign?

(A) To inform people where information can be obtained

(B) To remind people not to waste food

(C) To let people know where food can be purchased

(D) To remind people to work hard

Section Two

I. Free Response (Writing)

Note: In this part, you may NOT move back and forth among questions.

Directions: You will be asked to write in Chinese in a variety of ways. In each case, you will be asked to write for a specific purpose and to a specific person. You should write in as complete and as culturally appropriate a manner as possible, taking into account the purpose and the person described.

1. Story Narration

The four pictures present a story. Imagine you are writing the story to a friend. Narrate a complete story as suggested by the pictures. Give your story a beginning, a middle, and an end.

2. Personal Letter

Imagine you received a letter from a pen pal who lives in Beijing. In the letter he asks how the United States, as a nation of immigrants, treats its own culture and how the American culture was created in light of that fact. Write a letter in reply. Tell your pen pal what you think about the immigrant-based culture in the United States.

3. E-Mail Response

Read this e-mail from a friend and then type a response.

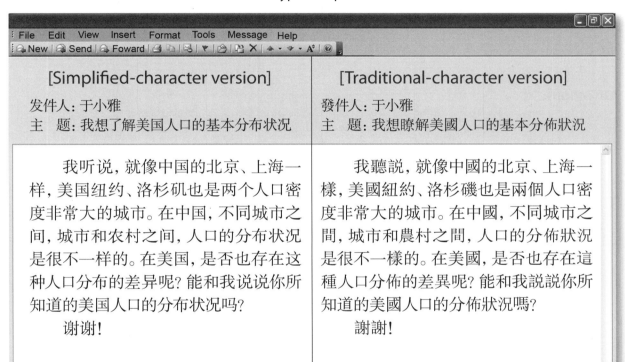

File　Edit　View　Insert　Format　Tools　Message　Help
New　Send　Foward

[Simplified-character version]

发件人: 于小雅
主　题: 我想了解美国人口的基本分布状况

　　我听说，就像中国的北京、上海一样，美国纽约、洛杉矶也是两个人口密度非常大的城市。在中国，不同城市之间，城市和农村之间，人口的分布状况是很不一样的。在美国，是否也存在这种人口分布的差异呢? 能和我说说你所知道的美国人口的分布状况吗?

　　谢谢!

[Traditional-character version]

發件人: 于小雅
主　題: 我想瞭解美國人口的基本分佈狀況

　　我聽説，就像中國的北京、上海一樣，美國紐約、洛杉磯也是兩個人口密度非常大的城市。在中國，不同城市之間，城市和農村之間，人口的分佈狀況是很不一樣的。在美國，是否也存在這種人口分佈的差異呢? 能和我説説你所知道的美國人口的分佈狀況嗎?

　　謝謝!

4. Relay a Telephone Message

Your roommate has a friend who has not been attending school because he has been ill. He calls your roommate and you hear his voice message on the answering machine. You will listen twice to the message. Then relay the message, including the important details, by typing an e-mail to your friend.

II. Free Response (Speaking)

Note: In this part, you may NOT move back and forth among questions.

Directions: You will participate in a simulated conversation. Each time it is your turn to speak, you will have 20 seconds to record. You should respond as fully and as appropriately as possible.

1. Conversation

Imagine you are visiting your Chinese friend, Chang Peng. You have a conversation with his mother.

Directions: You will be asked to speak in Chinese on different topics in the following two questions. In each case, imagine you are making an oral presentation to your class or your family in Chinese. First, you will read and hear the topic for your presentation. You will have 4 minutes to prepare your presentation. Then you will have 2 minutes to record your presentation. Your presentation should be as complete as possible..

2. Cultural Presentation

In your presentation, talk about your understanding of the basic rules of etiquette concerning the way people treat each other in China. For example, how one gives a gift, how one treats his guests, etc. Elaborate on the details of these practices as you understand them to be and comment on their cultural significance. You may also make simple comparisons between such practices and those in the United States.

3. Event Plan

Choose a topic that you are interested in and design an exploratory learning activity that will enable you to conduct research on the topic. In your presentation to the class, talk about this activity, and elaborate on the topic you wish to explore, the possible methods you intend to use, and the objective of your activity. You should also explain some of the steps you intend to take and what you would prepare for the study.

UNIT SEVEN
LESSON 14
People and Society
Moving into a Modern Apartment

Section One

I. Multiple Choice (Listen to the dialogs)

Note: In this part, you may NOT move back and forth among questions.

Directions: In this part, you will hear several short conversations or parts of conversations followed by four choices, designated (A), (B), (C), and (D). Choose the one that continues or completes the conversation in a logical and culturally appropriate manner. You will have 5 seconds to answer each question.

1.	(A)	(B)	(C)	(D)	5.	(A)	(B)	(C)	(D)
2.	(A)	(B)	(C)	(D)	6.	(A)	(B)	(C)	(D)
3.	(A)	(B)	(C)	(D)	7.	(A)	(B)	(C)	(D)
4.	(A)	(B)	(C)	(D)	8.	(A)	(B)	(C)	(D)

II. Multiple Choice (Listen to the selections)

Note: In this part, you may move back and forth only among the questions associated with the current listening selection.

Directions: In this part, you will listen to several selections in Chinese. For each selection, you will be told whether it will be played once or twice. You may take notes as you listen. After listening to each selection, you will see questions in English. For each question, choose the response that is best according to the selection. You will have 12 seconds to answer each question.

Selection 1

1. Whose wedding did the woman attend?
   - (A) Her sister's
   - (B) Her sister's classmate's
   - (C) Her classmate's
   - (D) Her classmate's sister's

2. How old was the bride?

(A) Less than 30 years old   (B) 30 years old

(C) Over 30 years old   (D) Over 40 years old

3. According to the conversation, which of the following statements is TRUE?

(A) People nowadays want to marry young.

(B) If the father has good fortune, he will have many children.

(C) Having many children can bring about greater prosperity.

(D) In the past, people used to think that having many children would bring them happiness.

4. What does "丁克家庭（丁克家庭）" mean?

(A) A couple that married young

(B) A couple that married late in life

(C) A couple with many children

(D) A couple that chooses not to have children

Selection 2

5. Where are the students?

(A) At a manufacturer of children's food products

(B) At a dairy company

(C) At a cattle farm

(D) At a food supermarket

6. How many people work there?

(A) Over 10,000   (B) 50,000

(C) Over 100   (D) Over 40

7. Where are the products sold to?

(A) International markets

(B) Many provinces and cities

(C) Within the local province

(D) Places in southern China

Selection 3

8. What is implied about the woman?

(A) She used to be poor.

(B) She is preparing to get married.

(C) She loves her parents very much.

(D) She is unhappy with her life now.

9. What does "大手大脚（大手大腳）" mean in the selection?

    (A) A person with big hands and feet

    (B) A charitable person

    (C) An extravagant person

    (D) A person with great strength

Selection 4

10. What is said about the man in the selection?

    (A) He works in Beijing.   **(B)** He makes a living by writing poems.

    (C) He is quite famous.   **(D)** He only likes to write poems.

11. What is implied about the woman?

    (A) She is the man's ex-girlfriend.

    (B) She is a friend of the man's father.

    (C) She is a poet.

    (D) She relies on her father's financial support.

12. What does the woman think about the man?

    (A) She thinks he is a spendthrift.

    (B) She thinks he is not good at writing.

    (C) She thinks he cannot make a living on his own.

    (D) She thinks he has too many hobbies.

Selection 5

13. Why were Yao Ming and Zhang Ziyi mentioned in the conversation?

    (A) Both are very famous.

    (B) Both are rich.

    (C) Both were included in a ranking.

    (D) Both have been working very hard for a living.

14. What does the man think the success of a singer depends on?

    (A) Capability   **(B)** Luck

    (C) Money   **(D)** Hard work

15. What can we infer at the end of the conversation?

    (A) Neither the man nor the woman compromised.

    (B) The man and the woman had a quarrel.

    (C) The man convinced the woman to take his point of view.

    (D) The woman convinced the man to take her point of view.

III. Multiple Choice (Reading)

Note: In this part, you may move back and forth among all the questions.

Directions: You will read several selections in Chinese. Each selection is accompanied by a number of questions in English. For each question, choose the response that is best according to the selection.

Read this letter.

[Simplified-character version]

玛丽:
    你好! 最近忙吗? 好久没和你联系了。
    我快毕业了, 最近在忙我的经济学论文。为了写论文, 前一段时间我进行了一些社会调查。我发现中国的休假制度对国民经济的发展起着非常重要的作用。中国有三个重要的节日——春节、"五·一"劳动节和"十·一"国庆节, 这些节日各有三天的法定假期, 人们总是把三天假期和前后的两个双休日放在一起休息, 这样, 每个节日都可以连续休息七天。人们往往利用这些长假去旅行, 游览各地的名胜古迹, 这给中国的旅游、交通、商业等行业带来了大量的经济收入。因此, 这三个长假被称为"黄金周"。
    我的论文就准备写假日经济。
        你也在忙着写论文吧, 祝你顺利!
                                汤姆
                                4月8日

[Traditional-character version]

瑪麗:
    你好! 最近忙嗎? 好久没和你聯繫了。
    我快畢業了, 最近在忙我的經濟學論文。爲了寫論文, 前一段時間我進行了一些社會調查。我發現中國的休假制度對國民經濟的發展起著非常重要的作用。中國有三個重要的節日——春節、"五·一"勞動節和"十·一"國慶節, 這些節日各有三天的法定假期, 人們總是把三天假期和前後的兩個雙休日放在一起休息, 這樣, 每個節日都可以連續休息七天。人們往往利用這些長假去旅行, 遊覽各地的名勝古蹟, 這給中國的旅遊、交通、商業等行業帶來了大量的經濟收入。因此, 這三個長假被稱爲"黄金週"。
    我的論文就準備寫假日經濟。
        你也在忙著寫論文吧, 祝你順利!
                                湯姆
                                4月8日

1. What is Tom's main purpose in writing this letter?

   (A) To tell Mary the main focus of his paper

   (B) To invite Mary to do social research together

   (C) To provide Mary with materials that she needs for her paper

   (D) To inform Mary that he will be going on a vacation soon

2. According to the letter, how many official public holidays are there for each major festival?

   (A) 2 days

   (B) 3 days

   (C) 4 days

   (D) 7 days

3. What does "黄金周（黃金週）" mean?

   (A) An object that can bring people good luck

   (B) A special week when gold accessories are cheap

   (C) A duration when people can make a lot of money

   (D) A period that may bring great financial benefit to the country

Read this passage.

[Simplified-character version]	[Traditional-character version]
有一次，一位经济学家到外地参观，他站在一具恐龙化石前，对身边的游客说："这只恐龙的岁数足足有20亿年零10个月了。"游客非常惊讶，恭敬地问道："您是从哪里得到如此准确的信息的？"　经济学家不无自豪地回答说："10个月前我来这里参观过，那时讲解员告诉我这只恐龙已经20亿岁了。"	有一次，一位經濟學家到外地參觀，他站在一具恐龍化石前，對身邊的遊客說："這隻恐龍的歲數足足有20億年零10個月了。"遊客非常驚訝，恭敬地問道："您是從哪裏得到如此準確的信息的？"經濟學家不無自豪地回答說："10個月前我來這裏參觀過，那時講解員告訴我這隻恐龍已經20億歲了。"

4. Why was the tourist surprised?

   (A) He met an economist.

   (B) He had never seen dinosaur fossils before.

   (C) The dinosaur was 2 billion years old.

   (D) He was told the exact age of the dinosaur.

5. What kind of expression would the economist most likely have at that time?

   (A) Depressed

   (B) Smug

   (C) Angry

   (D) Doubtful

6. According to the passage, which of the following statements is TRUE?

   (A) Both the tourist and the economist are great fans of dinosaurs.

   (B) The economist was in the archaeology team which discovered the dinosaur fossils.

   (C) The economist visited the site recently.

   (D) The tourist was doubtful of what the economist said.

Read this information.

[Simplified-character version]	[Traditional-character version]
问卷调查	**問卷調查**
夏日来临,空调市场异常火爆。谁是最新的空调明星?谁将成为消费者的最佳选择?2006年4月15日至4月20日,《新繁报》邀请您参与调查,请于4月20日前将调查问卷寄至《新繁报》报社或登录《新繁报》网站"2006年度北京空调市场消费者有奖问卷调查"栏目,进行网上投票。本调查问卷结果及中奖名单将在4月21日的《新繁报》上公布。	夏日來臨,空調市場異常火爆。誰是最新的空調明星?誰將成爲消費者的最佳選擇?2006年4月15日至4月20日,《新繁報》邀請您參與調查,請於4月20日前將調查問卷寄至《新繁報》報社或登錄《新繁報》網站"2006年度北京空調市場消費者有獎問卷調查"欄目,進行網上投票。本調查問卷結果及中獎名單將在4月21日的《新繁報》上公佈。
奖项设置如下:	獎項設置如下:
一等奖1名 ：将获得价值1520元的手机一部。	一等獎1名 ：將獲得價值1520元的手機一部。
二等奖2名 ：将获得价值800元的音箱一对。	二等獎2名 ：將獲得價值800元的音箱一對。
三等奖10名：将获得价值268元的茶叶礼盒一个。	三等獎10名：將獲得價值268元的茶葉禮盒一個。

7. What does "谁是最新的空调明星(誰是最新的空調明星)" refer to?

   (A) The latest brand of air conditioner

   (B) The brand of air conditioner endorsed by a celebrity

   (C) The most popular brand of air conditioner at the present time

   (D) The celebrity who recently shot an advertisement for a brand of air conditioner

8. Participants can take part in the survey in _____ ways.

   (A) one

   (B) two

   (C) three

   (D) four

9.   How can people learn about the survey results?

(A)   By sending an e-mail to the newspaper

(B)   By making a telephone call to the newspaper

(C)   By checking on the Internet

(D)   By reading the newspaper

Read this fable.

[Simplified-character version]	[Traditional-character version]
有一天，动物们决定建立一所学校，学习的课程有：飞行、跑步、游泳和爬树等，要求动物一律要修满全部课程。 　鸭子游泳技术一流，飞行课成绩也不错，就是跑步不行。于是它放弃了游泳课，专练跑步，鸭掌都磨破了，可是跑步还是不及格，游泳技术也变得平平了。 　兔子在跑步课上是第一名，可是游泳时却下不了水。松鼠爬树最拿手，可是在飞行课上老师要求必须从地面飞起，而松鼠从树上往下跳，不算成绩。小鹰是问题儿童，在爬树课上，第一个到了树顶，但是完全不符合老师的要求。 　学期结束时，只有一条怪异的鳗鱼游泳成绩最好，而且勉强能飞能跑能爬，于是获得了各科平均最高分，成为全校第一名。	有一天，動物們決定建立一所學校，學習的課程有：飛行、跑步、游泳和爬樹等，要求動物一律要修滿全部課程。 　鴨子游泳技術一流，飛行課成績也不錯，就是跑步不行。於是牠放棄了游泳課，專練跑步，鴨掌都磨破了，可是跑步還是不及格，游泳技術也變得平平了。 　兔子在跑步課上是第一名，可是游泳時卻下不了水。松鼠爬樹最拿手，可是在飛行課上老師要求必須從地面飛起，而松鼠從樹上往下跳，不算成績。小鷹是問題兒童，在爬樹課上，第一個到了樹頂，但是完全不符合老師的要求。 　學期結束時，只有一條怪異的鰻魚游泳成績最好，而且勉強能飛能跑能爬，於是獲得了各科平均最高分，成爲全校第一名。

10.   According to the passage, which of the following statements is TRUE?

(A)   The way the eaglet climbed the tree did not meet the teacher's requirements.

(B)   The eel swam poorly.

(C)   The duck scored the worst for flying.

(D)   The squirrel did not attend the flying lesson.

11. How did the eel come in first in the entire school?

(A) It obtained excellent results for all the tests.

(B) The teacher loved it.

(C) It was most popular.

(D) It obtained the highest average score for all segments.

12. What does the school for animals aim to do?

(A) It aims to train every animal to master different skills.

(B) It aims to train different animals to master one important skill.

(C) It aims to teach the animals according to their natural talents.

(D) It aims to focus on the education of the young.

Read this passage.

[Simplified-character version]	[Traditional-character version]
在大学里,我们常常看到老师在课前擦黑板,为自己授课"清理战场"。为此,我们采访了一些学生。有的学生说:"我一次黑板也没擦过,不好意思在同学面前擦黑板。"有的说:"擦黑板会弄脏手,老师反正要写字,弄脏手没关系。"	在大學裏,我們常常看到老師在課前擦黑板,爲自己授課"清理戰場"。爲此,我們採訪了一些學生。有的學生説:"我一次黑板也没擦過,不好意思在同學面前擦黑板。"有的説:"擦黑板會弄髒手,老師反正要寫字,弄髒手没關係。"
大多数学生认为学生应该帮助老师擦黑板,但是很多同学没有擦过黑板,因为他们觉得总有一些学生干部或比较活跃的同学会去做。	大多數學生認爲學生應該幫助老師擦黑板,但是很多同學没有擦過黑板,因爲他們覺得總有一些學生幹部或比較活躍的同學會去做。
老师是什么看法呢? 北京大学的张老师说,黑板写满了字,老师、学生都可以擦,不必严格分工。清华大学李老师说,他不在乎学生擦不擦黑板,"重要的是让他们掌握所学的内容"。	老師是什麼看法呢? 北京大學的張老師説,黑板寫滿了字,老師、學生都可以擦,不必嚴格分工。清華大學李老師説,他不在乎學生擦不擦黑板,"重要的是讓他們掌握所學的内容"。

13. According to the passage, which of the following statements is TRUE?

(A) Some students are too shy to erase the blackboard in front of their classmates.

(B) Some student leaders do not want to help erase the blackboard.

(C) Some students feel that those students who are on duty that day should erase the blackboard.

(D) Some students are angry about being asked to erase the blackboard.

14. According to the passage, what kind of students may volunteer to help the teacher erase the blackboard?

    (A) Students who are more introverted

    (B) Students whose hands are already dirty

    (C) Students who are active

    (D) Students who are attentive

15. Which of the following statements does NOT represent the teachers' opinion?

    (A) It does not matter whether or not students erase the blackboard.

    (B) Both teachers and students may erase the blackboard.

    (C) Erasing the blackboard may dirty one's hands.

    (D) The most important thing is that students understand their studies.

Read this passage.

[Simplified-character version]	[Traditional-character version]
一个三代同堂的家庭刚买了一个新房子。两位老人在想怎么把原来的旧家具搬进新房子, 而年轻的夫妻则天天逛家具店。年轻的主张: "除了人是旧的, 剩下的全要新的。"老的说小的是败家子, 小的怪老的不开化。现在的年轻人能挣会花, 在他们看来, 旧的不去, 新的不来; 而老一代人节约惯了, 什么都舍不得扔掉, 觉得"早晚用得上"。还好第三代人还不会说话, 否则就会有更大的矛盾了。	一個三代同堂的家庭剛買了一個新房子。兩位老人在想怎麼把原來的舊家具搬進新房子, 而年輕的夫妻則天天逛家具店。年輕的主張: "除了人是舊的, 剩下的全要新的。"老的說小的是敗家子, 小的怪老的不開化。現在的年輕人能挣會花, 在他們看來, 舊的不去, 新的不來; 而老一代人節約慣了, 什麼都捨不得扔掉, 覺得"早晚用得上"。還好第三代人還不會說話, 否則就會有更大的矛盾了。

16. What is the main conflict between the elderly and the young?

    (A) How to deal with old furniture

    (B) How to buy new furniture

    (C) How to allocate the rooms

    (D) How to deal with the old house

17. What does "旧的不去, 新的不来 (舊的不去, 新的不來)" mean in the passage?

    (A) If you do not take the old furniture to the store, you will not be able to exchange them for new furniture.

    (B) If you do not get rid of the old furniture, you will not be able to buy new ones.

    (C) If the elderly are not willing to give up their old opinions, the young people will not be able to insist on their new opinions.

    (D) If the elderly are not willing to move out of the old house, the young people will not be able to move in to the new house.

18. What does "败家子 (敗家子)" mean in the passage?

    (A) It refers to young people who do not know how to take care of others.

    (B) It refers to young people who do not understand the elderly.

    (C) It refers to young people who do not know how to manage a household.

    (D) It refers to young people who are not conscientious in what they do.

19. Why is it said that if the third generation could speak, there might be even greater conflicts?

    (A) The third generation is indulgent.

    (B) The third generation will have different ideas.

    (C) The third generation needs bigger houses.

    (D) The third generation is able to earn and spend a lot of money.

Read this passage.

[Simplified-character version]	[Traditional-character version]
在北京要想寻找一些生活信息, 你可以使用北京网通的 "电话导航"。只要拨114, 衣食住行, 处处都能给您提供方便。预定机票、车票, 订酒店、饭店, 找房地产信息、商场、超市以及搬家服务信息等等, 无论新旧信息都可以找到, 而且不只给您一个选择, 后面还跟着一大串备选信息呢! 总之, 事无巨细, 用 "电话导航" ——114, 一查就知道啦!	在北京要想尋找一些生活信息, 你可以使用北京網通的 "電話導航"。只要撥114, 衣食住行, 處處都能給您提供方便。預定機票、車票, 訂酒店、飯店, 找房地產信息、商場、超市以及搬家服務信息等等, 無論新舊信息都可以找到, 而且不只給您一個選擇, 後面還跟着一大串備選信息呢! 總之, 事無巨細, 用 "電話導航" ——114, 一查就知道啦!

20. This passage is probably _____ .

    (A) a job advertisement

    (B) an advertisement

    (C) a telephone message

    (D) an activity notification form

21. According to the passage, under what circumstances should one dial "114"?

    (A) When one finds his house is on fire.

    (B) When one needs help during an emergency.

    (C) When one needs to rent an apartment.

    (D) When one finds his watch is stolen.

Read this public sign.

    [Simplified-character version]   [Traditional-character version]

<table>
<tr><td>游人止步</td><td>遊人止步</td></tr>
</table>

22. Where would this sign most likely appear?

    (A) Beside a swimming pool

    (B) In a park

    (C) In a shopping mall

    (D) In a hospital

23. What does this sign mean?

    (A) This area is restricted.

    (B) No running is permitted.

    (C) No swimming is allowed beyond this point.

    (D) The path ahead is slippery.

Read this public sign.

    [Simplified-character version]   [Traditional-character version]

<table>
<tr><td>外币兑换处</td><td>外幣兌換處</td></tr>
</table>

24. Where would this sign most likely appear?

    (A) In a post office

    (B) In an airport

    (C) In an office

    (D) In a school

25. What does this sign mean?

    (A) People can buy things here.

    (B) People can make telephone calls here.

    (C) People can deposit money here.

    (D) People can exchange currency here.

Section Two

I. Free Response (Writing)

Note: In this part, you may NOT move back and forth among questions.

Directions: You will be asked to write in Chinese in a variety of ways. In each case, you will be asked to write for a specific purpose and to a specific person. You should write in as complete and as culturally appropriate a manner as possible, taking into account the purpose and the person described.

1. Story Narration

The four pictures present a story. Imagine you are writing the story to a friend. Narrate a complete story as suggested by the pictures. Give your story a beginning, a middle, and an end.

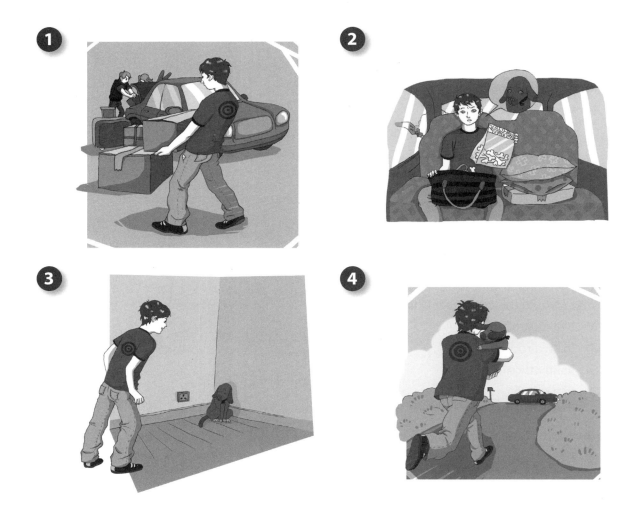

2. Personal Letter

Imagine you received a letter from a pen pal in Beijing. In the letter, he says he and his classmates have been discussing what social issues are most deserving of attention in present-day China. Write a reply in letter format. Tell your pen pal what you think about the social issues that demand urgent attention in the United States.

3. E-Mail Response

Read this e-mail from a friend and then type a response.

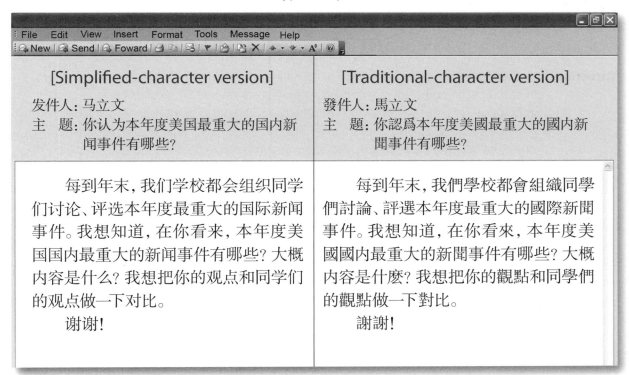

| File   Edit   View   Insert   Format   Tools   Message   Help |
| New   Send   Foward |

[Simplified-character version]	[Traditional-character version]
发件人: 马立文 主　题: 你认为本年度美国最重大的国内新闻事件有哪些?	發件人: 馬立文 主　題: 你認爲本年度美國最重大的國内新聞事件有哪些?
每到年末,我们学校都会组织同学们讨论、评选本年度最重大的国际新闻事件。我想知道,在你看来,本年度美国国内最重大的新闻事件有哪些? 大概内容是什么? 我想把你的观点和同学们的观点做一下对比。 　　谢谢!	每到年末,我們學校都會組織同學們討論、評選本年度最重大的國際新聞事件。我想知道,在你看來,本年度美國國内最重大的新聞事件有哪些? 大概内容是什麽? 我想把你的觀點和同學們的觀點做一下對比。 　　謝謝!

4. Relay a Telephone Message

Your family will soon be moving. Your mother has made an appointment with a moving company. They call your mother and you hear the message on the answering machine. You will listen to the message twice. Then relay the message, including the important details, by typing a note to your mother.

II. Free Response (Speaking)

Note: In this part, you may NOT move back and forth among questions.

Directions: You will participate in a simulated conversation. Each time it is your turn to speak, you will have 20 seconds to record. You should respond as fully and as appropriately as possible.

1. Conversation

Imagine you are studying in China. You want to rent an apartment and you turn to a real estate service agency for help. You have a conversation with a staff member at the agency.

Directions: You will be asked to speak in Chinese on different topics in the following two questions. In each case, imagine you are making an oral presentation to your class or your family in Chinese. First, you will read and hear the topic for your presentation. You will have 4 minutes to prepare your presentation. Then you will have 2 minutes to record your presentation. Your presentation should be as complete as possible.

2. Cultural Presentation

In your presentation, talk about what you know about traditional Chinese architecture, and discuss its distinctive characteristics and the Chinese cultural values embodied in them.

3. Event Plan

Imagine you are the principal of a school. Plan the school curriculum and explain it to your colleagues. In your presentation, you should state clearly the purpose of your plan, your objectives, the main features, and some possible advantages and disadvantages.

UNIT EIGHT
LESSON 15
Chinese Language and Characters
Characters Relating to Animals

Section One

I. Multiple Choice (Listen to the dialogs)

Note: In this part, you may NOT move back and forth among questions.

Directions: In this part, you will hear several short conversations or parts of conversations followed by four choices, designated (A), (B), (C), and (D). Choose the one that continues or completes the conversation in a logical and culturally appropriate manner. You will have 5 seconds to answer each question.

1.	(A)	(B)	(C)	(D)	5.	(A)	(B)	(C)	(D)
2.	(A)	(B)	(C)	(D)	6.	(A)	(B)	(C)	(D)
3.	(A)	(B)	(C)	(D)	7.	(A)	(B)	(C)	(D)
4.	(A)	(B)	(C)	(D)	8.	(A)	(B)	(C)	(D)

II. Multiple Choice (Listen to the selections)

Note: In this part, you may move back and forth only among the questions associated with the current listening selection.

Directions: In this part, you will listen to several selections in Chinese. For each selection, you will be told whether it will be played once or twice. You may take notes as you listen. After listening to each selection, you will see questions in English. For each question, choose the response that is best according to the selection. You will have 12 seconds to answer each question.

Selection 1

1. How many sets of books did the speaker introduce in her speech?
   - (A) One set
   - (B) Two sets
   - (C) Three sets
   - (D) Four sets

2. Why did the publishing house publish these books?

   (A) Chinese characters are interesting.

   (B) Many people want to learn Chinese.

   (C) There are many ways to learn Chinese characters.

   (D) Chinese characters are difficult to learn.

3. According to the speaker, what is a feature of《汉字ABC》(《漢字ABC》)?

   (A) It is very interesting.

   (B) It deals with the basic characteristics of Chinese characters.

   (C) It teaches how to memorize Chinese characters.

   (D) It is very systematic.

Selection 2

4. Which Chinese character does this man NOT know?

   (A) "惊（驚）"

   (B) "谅（諒）"

   (C) "亮（亮）"

   (D) "京（京）"

5. According to the conversation, why are "谅（諒）" and "惊（驚）" pronounced differently?

   (A) They have different meanings.

   (B) They have different character components.

   (C) Chinese character forms have changed greatly.

   (D) Pronunciation of Chinese characters has changed greatly.

6. According to the conversation, which of the following statements is TRUE?

   (A) For all Chinese characters, one of its components indicates the pronunciation of the whole character.

   (B) Chinese characters with the same character component have the same meaning.

   (C) "京（京）" has never been an indication of the pronunciation of "谅（諒）".

   (D) Some Chinese characters with the same character component are pronounced quite differently.

Selection 3

7. Who named the baby?

   (A) The father's parents

   (B) The parents

   (C) The mother's parents

   (D) The mother's friend

8. Why is the name "张雷（張雷）" unacceptable?

   (A) There are too many people with that name.

   (B) It is difficult to write.

   (C) It has an unpleasant sound.

   (D) It does not have a good meaning.

9. What is the main purpose of the woman's call?

   (A) She wants Xiao Yan to help her think of a name.

   (B) She wants to thank Xiao Yan for giving her baby a name.

   (C) She wants to tell Xiao Yan that her baby's name is "张明（張明）".

   (D) She wants Xiao Yan to return her call.

Selection 4

10. What kind of mistake does the woman frequently make?

    (A) She often writes Chinese characters incorrectly.

    (B) She often uses wrong Chinese phrases.

    (C) She often pronounces Chinese characters incorrectly.

    (D) She often makes mistakes in listening comprehension.

11. What is the woman's family name?

    (A) "柏（柏）" **(B)** "白（白）"

    (C) "百（百）" **(D)** "伯（伯）"

12. Why does the man say that the woman's teachers must be very handsome?

    (A) The woman's teachers are really very handsome.

    (B) The man is laughing at the woman's teachers.

    (C) The man is laughing at the woman's mistake of writing the wrong character.

    (D) The man admires the woman's teachers very much.

Selection 5

13. According to the method mentioned, what is the first step in looking up a Chinese character in a dictionary?

    (A) Determine the basic radical of the character

    (B) Locate the page in the radical index where the character appears

    (C) Look for the page where the character appears in the dictionary

    (D) Determine how the character is pronounced

14. What is most probably the speaker's occupation?

    (A) Salesperson **(B)** Bookstore assistant

    (C) Teacher **(D)** Student

III. Multiple Choice (Reading)

Note: In this part, you may move back and forth among all the questions.

Directions: You will read several selections in Chinese. Each selection is accompanied by a number of questions in English. For each question, choose the response that is best according to the selection.

Read this e-mail.

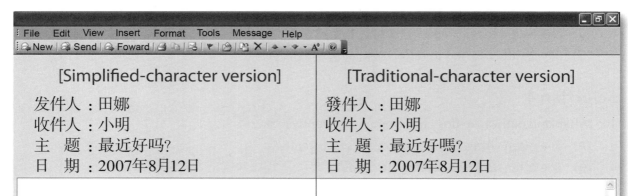

[Simplified-character version]	[Traditional-character version]
发件人：田娜	發件人：田娜
收件人：小明	收件人：小明
主　题：最近好吗?	主　題：最近好嗎?
日　期：2007年8月12日	日　期：2007年8月12日

小明:

你好!

很长时间没给你写信了, 真不好意思! 国庆节这七天长假, 你出去玩了吗?

这个假期我哪儿也没去, 一直在宿舍里学习。因为一上二年级, 我就发现学习内容难了很多, 一天就要学好多生字。刚开学的时候, 我觉得非常吃力, 几乎都要放弃了。我问老师, 可不可以不学汉字? 老师说, 对一个中文专业的大学生来说, 非学汉字不可, 因为不学的话, 就是个文盲, 既不能读中文报纸, 也不能读中文书籍。老师还说, 汉字不仅记录了汉语, 还记录了中国的文化和历史, 坚持学下去, 就能逐渐感受到它的魅力。其实我在一年级的时候, 也觉得汉字很有意思。可能是现在压力有点大, 才会有这样的想法。

赶快给我回信, 告诉我你的近况吧!

田娜

小明:

你好!

很長時間沒給你寫信了, 真不好意思! 國慶節這七天長假, 你出去玩了嗎?

這個假期我哪兒也沒去, 一直在宿舍裏學習。因爲一上二年級, 我就發現學習內容難了很多, 一天就要學好多生字。剛開學的時候, 我覺得非常吃力, 幾乎都要放棄了。我問老師, 可不可以不學漢字? 老師說, 對一個中文專業的大學生來說, 非學漢字不可, 因爲不學的話, 就是個文盲, 既不能讀中文報紙, 也不能讀中文書籍。老師還說, 漢字不僅記錄了漢語, 還記錄了中國的文化和歷史, 堅持學下去, 就能逐漸感受到它的魅力。其實我在一年級的時候, 也覺得漢字很有意思。可能是現在壓力有點大, 才會有這樣的想法。

趕快給我回信, 告訴我你的近況吧!

田娜

1. What did Tian Na do during the National Day holiday?
   (A) She went on a trip.
   (B) She went to visit her parents.
   (C) She stayed in the dormitory to study.
   (D) She spent the time reading Chinese storybooks.

2. What is Tian Na's major and which year of study is she in?
   (A) Chinese, freshman
   (B) Chinese, sophomore
   (C) History, freshman
   (D) History, sophomore

3. What main difficulty did Tian Na encounter in her studies this term?
   (A) There are too many grammatical points to learn.
   (B) There are too many new characters to learn.
   (C) She has difficulty understanding the Chinese newspapers.
   (D) She has difficulty understanding Chinese history and culture.

Read this notice.

[Simplified-character version]	[Traditional-character version]

2008年书法辅导班招生简章

为普及书法知识，我院书法专业决定今年寒假继续开办书法辅导班。具体事宜如下：

一、教学内容
1. 由××大学艺术与传媒学院书法专业教师讲授书法知识、答疑并进行具体书写指导。
2. 组织学院书法专业的优秀学生对辅导班学员进行辅导。

二、课程安排
1. 书法基础知识；
2. 书法创作理论与实践。

三、上课时间
2008年2月1日—18日，共15天。其中春节休息3天（2月7日—9日）。

四、报名方法
即日起开始报名，来函报名、电话报名均可。来校报到时请带身份证和一寸照片一张。纸张、笔墨自备。我们尽力帮助联系安排外地学生的食宿，费用自理。

五、上课地点
××大学艺术楼601教室

六、联系方式
××大学艺术系
书法教研室，邮编：100875
咨询电话：（010）38105557
办公室电话：（010）38102046

××大学艺术与传媒学院书法专业
2007年12月20日

2008年書法輔導班招生簡章

爲普及書法知識，我院書法專業決定今年寒假繼續開辦書法輔導班。具體事宜如下：

一、教學內容
1. 由××大學藝術與傳媒學院書法專業教師講授書法知識、答疑並進行具體書寫指導。
2. 組織學院書法專業的優秀學生對輔導班學員進行輔導。

二、課程安排
1. 書法基礎知識；
2. 書法創作理論與實踐。

三、上課時間
2008年2月1日—18日，共15天。其中春節休息3天（2月7日—9日）。

四、報名方法
即日起開始報名，來函報名、電話報名均可。來校報到時請帶身份證和一寸照片一張。紙張、筆墨自備。我們盡力幫助聯繫安排外地學生的食宿，費用自理。

五、上課地點
××大學藝術樓601教室

六、聯繫方式
××大學藝術系
書法教研室，郵編：100875
諮詢電話：（010）38105557
辦公室電話：（010）38102046

××大學藝術與傳媒學院書法專業
2007年12月20日

4. Which of the following is NOT required of the teachers in this class?

   (A) Answering questions

   (B) Teaching specialized knowledge

   (C) Guiding the students in writing

   (D) Providing counseling services

5. According to the notice, which of the following statements is TRUE?

   (A) This is the first time that the calligraphy class is being offered.

   (B) The location of the class has not been confirmed.

   (C) Students attending the class must bring along their own paper and ink.

   (D) The only way to register for this class is by calling the office.

Read this passage.

[Simplified-character version]	[Traditional-character version]
以前，中国人喜欢用毛笔写字，并逐渐形成了书法艺术。随着钢笔、圆珠笔等新的书写工具的出现，人们早已不用毛笔写字了，而这种传统艺术也就渐渐衰落了。在电脑技术日益发展的今天，"无笔书写"又在某种程度上替代了"硬笔（钢笔、圆珠笔）书写"，几乎连字都不用"写"了，更不用说"书法"艺术了。甚至还有人预言，电脑的发展会把"书法"送进历史博物馆。但也有的学者认为，要努力抢救书法，保护这种具有中国特色的艺术形式。因此，我们建议，要规定中小学生、读文史的大专学生乃至部分政府公务员学写毛笔字，以适当扩大书法的群众基础；同时还应该建设优秀的专业、业余书法家队伍等等。	以前，中國人喜歡用毛筆寫字，並逐漸形成了書法藝術。隨着鋼筆、圓珠筆等新的書寫工具的出現，人們早已不用毛筆寫字了，而這種傳統藝術也就漸漸衰落了。在電腦技術日益發展的今天，"無筆書寫"又在某種程度上替代了"硬筆（鋼筆、圓珠筆）書寫"，幾乎連字都不用"寫"了，更不用說"書法"藝術了。甚至還有人預言，電腦的發展會把"書法"送進歷史博物館。但也有的學者認爲，要努力搶救書法，保護這種具有中國特色的藝術形式。因此，我們建議，要規定中小學生、讀文史的大專學生乃至部分政府公務員學寫毛筆字，以適當擴大書法的群衆基礎；同時還應該建設優秀的專業、業餘書法家隊伍等等。

6. According to the passage, why has traditional calligraphy become less popular?

   (A) Writing instruments have changed.

   (B) Fewer people like to practice calligraphy.

   (C) People's views toward calligraphy have changed.

   (D) Chinese characters are too difficult to write.

7. What does "电脑的发展会把 '书法' 送进历史博物馆 (電腦的發展會把 '書法' 送進歷史博物館)" mean?

(A) Traditional calligraphy may disappear.

(B) Writing instruments should be exhibited.

(C) Computers can preserve works of calligraphy.

(D) Works of calligraphy should be exhibited.

8. How does the author feel about the changes that threaten the survival of traditional calligraphy?

(A) He thinks that the changes reflect a degeneration of society.

(B) He rejects the changes completely.

(C) He accepts the changes with ease.

(D) He advocates the protection of the traditional art of calligraphy.

Read this passage.

[Simplified-character version]	[Traditional-character version]
汉字对周边国家的文化产生过巨大的影响,形成了一个"汉字文化圈"。在日本、越南和朝鲜半岛,曾经长时间地使用汉字。早在公元一世纪,汉字便传入了越南。后来,越南人在汉字的基础上创造了"字喃",直到1945年越南才废除汉字,完全改用拼音文字。而在朝鲜半岛,公元三世纪左右,汉字就已经传入了。那里的人们也曾经完全使用汉字来书写他们的语言。现在的韩国虽不再在正式场合中使用汉字,不过汉字在民间仍在继续使用。朝鲜在1948年废除汉字时,仍保留了若干汉字。大约也是在公元三世纪,汉字传入了日本。日语曾经完全用汉字来书写。二战后,日本开始限制汉字的数量,不过在许多情况下,汉字的使用并不受限制。	漢字對周邊國家的文化產生過巨大的影響,形成了一個"漢字文化圈"。在日本、越南和朝鮮半島,曾經長時間地使用漢字。早在公元一世紀,漢字便傳入了越南。後來,越南人在漢字的基礎上創造了"字喃",直到1945年越南才廢除漢字,完全改用拼音文字。而在朝鮮半島,公元三世紀左右,漢字就已經傳入了。那裏的人們也曾經完全使用漢字來書寫他們的語言。現在的韓國雖不再在正式場合中使用漢字,不過漢字在民間仍在繼續使用。朝鮮在1948年廢除漢字時,仍保留了若干漢字。大約也是在公元三世紀,漢字傳入了日本。日語曾經完全用漢字來書寫。二戰後,日本開始限制漢字的數量,不過在許多情況下,漢字的使用並不受限制。

9. Which of the following countries first adopted the use of Chinese characters?

(A) Japan

(B) Vietnam

(C) North Korea

(D) South Korea

10. According to the passage, one can no longer find any trace of Chinese characters in the writing system of _____ .

   (A) Japan
   (B) South Korea
   (C) Vietnam
   (D) North Korea

11. According to the passage, which of the following statement is NOT true?

   (A) Japan began to limit the use of Chinese characters after World War I.
   (B) Vietnam completely abolished the use of Chinese characters.
   (C) South Korea no longer uses Chinese characters on formal occasions.
   (D) "字喃（字喃）" is based on Chinese characters.

Read this passage.

[Simplified-character version]	[Traditional-character version]
常听人说：学汉语要有好的学习材料，还要练好基本功，把字、词、句掌握好。这些当然都不错，但是说好汉语和语言环境是分不开的，如果你到中国去学汉语，显然条件很好，不过如果你在中国学习，却不和别人交往，可能也不会有很大的进步。约翰是纽约一所中学的汉语老师，他从来没有到过中国，但是他有很多华人朋友，经常和他们用汉语聊天，他的汉语说得好极了。由此可见，虽然学汉语最好是在中国，但并不是在其他国家就肯定学不好，学习英语、法语或其他语言也是一样。	常聽人說：學漢語要有好的學習材料，還要練好基本功，把字、詞、句掌握好。這些當然都不錯，但是說好漢語和語言環境是分不開的，如果你到中國去學漢語，顯然條件很好，不過如果你在中國學習，卻不和別人交往，可能也不會有很大的進步。約翰是紐約一所中學的漢語老師，他從來沒有到過中國，但是他有很多華人朋友，經常和他們用漢語聊天，他的漢語說得好極了。由此可見，雖然學漢語最好是在中國，但並不是在其他國家就肯定學不好，學習英語、法語或其他語言也是一樣。

12. In the writer's opinion, what is the most important factor in learning Chinese?

   (A) One must live in China.
   (B) One must have good learning materials.
   (C) One must have a good language environment.
   (D) One must master Chinese characters, vocabulary, and grammar.

13. According to the passage, which of the following statements about John is TRUE?

   (A) He went to China to learn Chinese many years ago.
   (B) He can speak English, French, and many other languages.
   (C) He teaches Chinese in an elementary school in New York.
   (D) He often converses in Chinese with Chinese people.

14. What does "基本功（基本功）" mean in the passage?

(A) The ability to understand

(B) The knowledge of the language

(C) The learning environment

(D) The ability to articulate

Read this passage.

[Simplified-character version]

英国商人曾反映，"白象"牌电池出口英国后，很少有人购买。原来这种电池的商标翻译成英文是"White Elephant"，而"White Elephant"在英文中是花钱买废物的意思。这出自一个传说：古代泰国国王不喜欢某个大臣时，就送他一头白象，让他在家中精心喂养，弄得他钱财耗尽，痛苦万分，而白象本身却毫无用处。这就难怪英国人不愿掏钱买这种"没有实用价值"的电池了。

美国可口可乐公司近年推出了一种饮料，名叫"Sprite"，意思是"妖怪"。西方人觉得"妖怪"有趣好玩，可是如果直接翻译成中文，中国顾客肯定会望而生畏，谁还来买呢？然而"Sprite"进入中国后，有了一个美妙的商标——"雪碧"，获得了大家的喜爱。可见翻译不仅要考虑语言的形式或意义，更要考虑不同文化背景以及欣赏习惯的差异。

[Traditional-character version]

英國商人曾反映，"白象"牌電池出口英國後，很少有人購買。原來這種電池的商標翻譯成英文是"White Elephant"，而"White Elephant"在英文中是花錢買廢物的意思。這出自一個傳說：古代泰國國王不喜歡某個大臣時，就送他一頭白象，讓他在家中精心餵養，弄得他錢財耗盡，痛苦萬分，而白象本身卻毫無用處。這就難怪英國人不願掏錢買這種"沒有實用價值"的電池了。

美國可口可樂公司近年推出了一種飲料，名叫"Sprite"，意思是"妖怪"。西方人覺得"妖怪"有趣好玩，可是如果直接翻譯成中文，中國顧客肯定會望而生畏，誰還來買呢？然而"Sprite"進入中國後，有了一個美妙的商標——"雪碧"，獲得了大家的喜愛。可見翻譯不僅要考慮語言的形式或意義，更要考慮不同文化背景以及欣賞習慣的差異。

15. Why did the English people refuse to buy batteries named "白象（白象）"?

(A) Their quality was poor.

(B) They were too expensive.

(C) They were not durable.

(D) The name was not chosen well.

16. Why did the king of Thailand present a white elephant to his minister?

(A) The white elephant signifies prosperity.

(B) It is a tradition for the king to present gifts to ministers who have earned merit.

(C) The king wanted to test the minister's loyalty.

(D) The king wanted to torment a minister he did not like.

17. What does "雪碧 (雪碧)" remind people of?

(A) Cool ice and snow

(B) Hot summer

(C) Bright colors

(D) Fascinating spirits

18. Why was "Sprite" translated to "雪碧 (雪碧)"?

(A) "Sprite" has the same meaning as "雪碧 (雪碧)" in Chinese.

(B) The Chinese people like the English meaning of "Sprite".

(C) The Chinese people are superstitious.

(D) "Sprite" means "妖怪 (妖怪)" in Chinese.

Read this passage.

[Simplified-character version]	[Traditional-character version]
据统计，汉字中的形声字约占80%以上。形声字的特点是：形旁表义，声旁表音。如"访、纺、芳、房、妨、防、放、仿"这一组字，根据它们的声旁"方"，我们可以推测出它们的读音；根据形旁，我们可以知道每个字所表示的意义的类别。但是我们今天所看到的形声字，它们的声旁所表示的读音，往往与整个字的读音有些不同，如"尚"读"shàng"，但以"尚"为声旁的"躺"读"tǎng"，"党"读"dǎng"，"常"读"cháng"，"敞"读"chǎng"。这些是由于历史的演变造成的，因为语言的发展变化，有些形声字的表音功能逐渐减弱甚至丧失了。	據統計，漢字中的形聲字約佔80%以上。形聲字的特點是：形旁表義，聲旁表音。如"訪、紡、芳、房、妨、防、放、仿"這一組字，根據它們的聲旁"方"，我們可以推測出它們的讀音；根據形旁，我們可以知道每個字所表示的意義的類別。但是我們今天所看到的形聲字，它們的聲旁所表示的讀音，往往與整個字的讀音有些不同，如"尚"讀"shàng"，但以"尚"爲聲旁的"躺"讀"tǎng"，"黨"讀"dǎng"，"常"讀"cháng"，"敞"讀"chǎng"。這些是由於歷史的演變造成的，因爲語言的發展變化，有些形聲字的表音功能逐漸減弱甚至喪失了。

19. In the character "躺（躺）", which part is the pictographic element?

(A) 小（小）

(B) 回（回）

(C) 身（身）

(D) 尚（尚）

20. "芳（芳）" is a pictophonetic character. According to the characteristics of pictophonetic characters, we may infer that "芳（芳）" originally meant _____ .

(A) a square object

(B) a plant

(C) an odor

(D) beauty

21. Which of the following statements about the pictophonetic character is TRUE?

(A) It must comprise a phonetic element and a pictographic element.

(B) It has the same meaning as its pictographic element.

(C) The development of language did not affect the phonetic element.

(D) The pronunciation of the pictophonetic character is the same as its phonetic element.

Read this public sign.

[Simplified-character version]

热烈庆祝第十届大学生电影节开幕

[Traditional-character version]

熱烈慶祝第十屆大學生電影節開幕

22. Where would this sign most likely appear?

(A) On a school campus

(B) In a factory

(C) In a shopping mall

(D) In a hospital

23. What does "开幕（開幕）" in the sign mean?

(A) The screening of a movie

(B) The unveiling of the stage curtain

(C) The beginning of an activity

(D) The celebratory preparations

Read this public sign.

[Simplified-character version]

持卡人签名

[Traditional-character version]

持卡人簽名

24. Where would this sign most likely appear?

(A) On an exam paper

(B) On a bill

(C) On a student's identity card

(D) On a passport

25. What does it ask people to write?

(A) The name of the hotel

(B) The name of the school

(C) Their own names

(D) Their home addresses

Section Two

I. Free Response (Writing)

Note: In this part, you may NOT move back and forth among questions.

Directions: You will be asked to write in Chinese in a variety of ways. In each case, you will be asked to write for a specific purpose and to a specific person. You should write in as complete and as culturally appropriate a manner as possible, taking into account the purpose and the person described.

1. Story Narration

The four pictures present a story. Imagine you are writing the story to a friend. Narrate a complete story as suggested by the pictures. Give your story a beginning, a middle, and an end.

2. Personal Letter

Imagine you received a letter from a pen pal in Beijing. In the letter he asks your opinion about the significance and value of learning Chinese. Write a reply in letter format. Tell your pen pal what you think about the topic.

3. E-Mail Response

Read this e-mail from a friend and then type a response.

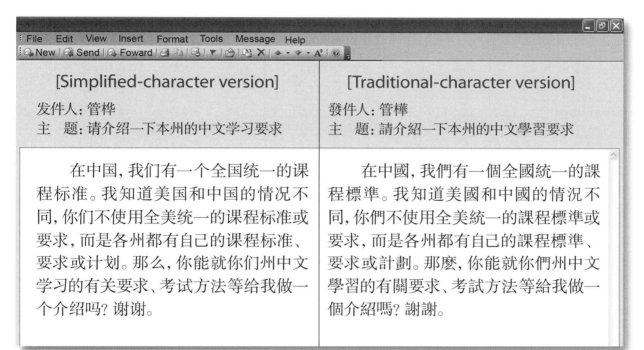

File Edit View Insert Format Tools Message Help

New | Send | Foward | | | | | | X | | |

[Simplified-character version]

发件人: 管桦
主　题: 请介绍一下本州的中文学习要求

　　在中国，我们有一个全国统一的课程标准。我知道美国和中国的情况不同，你们不使用全美统一的课程标准或要求，而是各州都有自己的课程标准、要求或计划。那么，你能就你们州中文学习的有关要求、考试方法等给我做一个介绍吗? 谢谢。

[Traditional-character version]

發件人: 管樺
主　題: 請介紹一下本州的中文學習要求

　　在中國，我們有一個全國統一的課程標準。我知道美國和中國的情況不同，你們不使用全美統一的課程標準或要求，而是各州都有自己的課程標準、要求或計劃。那麼，你能就你們州中文學習的有關要求、考試方法等給我做一個介紹嗎? 謝謝。

4. Relay a Telephone Message

An employee at a shopping mall calls your mother on the telephone. You will listen twice to the message. Then relay the message, including the important details, by typing a note to your mother.

II. Free Response (Speaking)

Note: In this part, you may NOT move back and forth among questions.

Directions: You will participate in a simulated conversation. Each time it is your turn to speak, you will have 20 seconds to record. You should respond as fully and as appropriately as possible.

1. Conversation

You are going to be a learning partner to a Chinese student. You will teach him English and he will teach you Chinese. You have a conversation with him.

Directions: You will be asked to speak in Chinese on different topics in the following two questions. In each case, imagine you are making an oral presentation to your class or your family in Chinese. First, you will read and hear the topic for your presentation. You will have 4 minutes to prepare your presentation. Then you will have 2 minutes to record your presentation. Your presentation should be as complete as possible.

2. Cultural Presentation

Using some Chinese characters that you are familiar with, like, and understand well as examples, talk about the basic characteristics of Chinese characters in your presentation. You may proceed in two ways. You may give some examples first, followed by a summary of the characteristics of Chinese characters. Alternatively, you may talk about your understanding and impression of Chinese characters first and then cite some examples.

3. Event Plan

You class is preparing to look for a sister class in China. In your presentation, talk about your thoughts and plans with regards to this activity. Include the channels and means you intend to use to locate the class. Describe the kind of class you hope to find and the mutually beneficial activities you plan to hold with your sister class in future.

UNIT EIGHT Chinese Language and Characters
LESSON 16 "Prosperity Has Arrived!"

Section One

I. Multiple Choice (Listen to the dialogs)

Note: In this part, you may NOT move back and forth among questions.

Directions: In this part, you will hear several short conversations or parts of conversations followed by four choices, designated (A), (B), (C), and (D). Choose the one that continues or completes the conversation in a logical and culturally appropriate manner. You will have 5 seconds to answer each question.

1.	(A)	(B)	(C)	(D)	5.	(A)	(B)	(C)	(D)
2.	(A)	(B)	(C)	(D)	6.	(A)	(B)	(C)	(D)
3.	(A)	(B)	(C)	(D)	7.	(A)	(B)	(C)	(D)
4.	(A)	(B)	(C)	(D)	8.	(A)	(B)	(C)	(D)

II. Multiple Choice (Listen to the selections)

Note: In this part, you may move back and forth only among the questions associated with the current listening selection.

Directions: In this part, you will listen to several selections in Chinese. For each selection, you will be told whether it will be played once or twice. You may take notes as you listen. After listening to each selection, you will see questions in English. For each question, choose the response that is best according to the selection. You will have 12 seconds to answer each question.

Selection 1

1. Where would this conversation most likely take place?
    (A) In a classroom
    (B) In a library
    (C) In a bookstore
    (D) In a publishing house

2. According to the conversation, which of the following information does the woman NOT need to provide?

(A) The date

(B) The name of the publishing house

(C) The title of the book

(D) The mode of contact

3. When will the dictionary most likely be available?

(A) In less than three days

(B) In three days at the earliest

(C) Within four days at the earliest

(D) In exactly three days

Selection 2

4. What is the most likely relationship between the speaker and Xiao Fang?

(A) Sisters

(B) Strangers

(C) Relatives

(D) Friends

5. Why did Xiao Fang leave without saying a word?

(A) She was tired that day.

(B) She did not want to borrow any more money.

(C) She was somewhat unhappy.

(D) She was too busy and did not have time to talk.

6. Which of the following explains why the woman said "我手头有点紧（我手頭有點緊）"?

(A) She does not have much money on hand.

(B) She has a lot of money on hand.

(C) She thinks a refusal should be expressed tactfully.

(D) She thinks one should quickly apologize for one's mistake.

Selection 3

7. What is the most likely relationship between Xiao Mei and the man who left this telephone message?

(A) Colleagues in an office

(B) Father and daughter

(C) Boyfriend and girlfriend

(D) Teacher and student

8. What is the purpose of the man's call?

(A) He wants to know how Xiao Mei is doing.

(B) He wants to invite Xiao Mei to dinner.

(C) He wants to introduce Xiao Mei to a Sichuan restaurant.

(D) He wants to ask if Xiao Mei has classes that evening.

9. Where will Xiao Mei and the man meet?

(A) At the entrance of the Sichuan restaurant

(B) At the entrance of the Japanese restaurant

(C) At the school gate

(D) At Xiao Mei's door

Selection 4

10. What did most of the guests at the party think about the child?

(A) They thought the child's replies were not very good.

(B) They thought the child's replies were very ordinary.

(C) They thought the child's replies were very good.

(D) They thought the child did not like to answer their questions.

11. What does "有出息（有出息）" mean in this narration?

(A) To have a promising future   (B) To work abroad in future

(C) To have an easy job   (D) To have time to rest

12. Why did the child say that the guest must have been very intelligent as a child?

(A) The child has heard some stories about the guest's childhood.

(B) The guest is very eloquent.

(C) The guest is very intelligent now.

(D) The child thought that the guest's remarks were rude.

Selection 5

13. What is the woman's impression of Xiamen?

(A) The traffic is inconvenient.

(B) The scenery is attractive.

(C) The city is big.

(D) There are many foreigners.

14. The man in the conversation is a _____.

(A) Southerner   (B) Northerner

(C) Japanese   (D) Westerner

15. According to the conversation, which of the following is NOT a reason for the existence of so many dialects in China?

(A) China is a big country.

(B) China has many ethnic groups.

(C) Travel in China used to be very inconvenient.

(D) The scope of Chinese people's lives used to be narrow.

III. Multiple Choice (Reading)

Note: In this part, you may move back and forth among all the questions.

Directions: You will read several selections in Chinese. Each selection is accompanied by a number of questions in English. For each question, choose the response that is best according to the selection.

Read this letter.

[Traditional-character version]

瑪麗:

你好!

你在來信中讓我猜猜這個謎語:"全國十二個,每人有一個。"我想了想,謎底應該是十二生肖。據說古時候的中國人爲了記住自己的出生年份,就找來了十二種動物表示十二個年份。而且不少人認爲,什麼年份出生的人一般會具有代表這個年份的動物的特點。就說我的一個朋友吧,她總和她的戀人鬧矛盾,動不動就説要分手,我問她爲什麼,她很無奈地說:"也許是因爲我們都是狗年出生的吧,聽説狗和狗在一起的時候比較容易打架。"

小新
10月5日

[Simplified-character version]

玛丽:

你好!

你在来信中让我猜猜这个谜语:"全国十二个,每人有一个。"我想了想,谜底应该是十二生肖。据说古时候的中国人为了记住自己的出生年份,就找来了十二种动物表示十二个年份。而且不少人认为,什么年份出生的人一般会具有代表这个年份的动物的特点。就说我的一个朋友吧,她总和她的恋人闹矛盾,动不动就说要分手,我问她为什么,她很无奈地说:"也许是因为我们都是狗年出生的吧,听说狗和狗在一起的时候比较容易打架。"

小新
10月5日

1. What is Xiao Xin's main purpose in writing this letter?

   (A) She is sharing with Ma Li her friend's relationship problems.

   (B) She wants to introduce Ma Li to Chinese astrology.

   (C) She is replying to Ma Li's letter.

   (D) She wants to give Ma Li a riddle.

2. According to the passage, why do people use the 12 zodiac animal signs?

   (A) They remind people of the year in which they were born.

   (B) All of the 12 animals are cute.

   (C) A person's personality is closely linked with his zodiac animal sign.

   (D) Each of the 12 zodiac animal signs has its own distinctive characteristics.

3. What does Xiao Xin's friend attribute her troubled relationship with her boyfriend to?

   (A) Her boyfriend does not have a good zodiac animal sign.

   (B) She does not like her boyfriend's zodiac animal sign.

   (C) Both of them were born in the year of the Dog.

   (D) Both of them quarrel easily.

Read this passage.

[Simplified-character version]	[Traditional-character version]
我有一个美国朋友，他是一个有名的音乐家。来中国演出的时候，他发现汉语听起来非常优美，于是对学习汉语产生了浓厚的兴趣。有一次，他听到一个中国人说"去方便一下"，就问我是什么意思，我告诉他，就是"去厕所"的意思。几天以后，他对我说，很多中国歌迷给他写信，可他实在太忙，不可能都回信。只有一封信让他很生气，所以他才回了信。那个歌迷说："请允许我在您方便的时候与您合影留念。"音乐家回信说："我在方便的时候从来不见客人。"	我有一個美國朋友，他是一個有名的音樂家。來中國演出的時候，他發現漢語聽起來非常優美，於是對學習漢語產生了濃厚的興趣。有一次，他聽到一個中國人說"去方便一下"，就問我是什麼意思，我告訴他，就是"去廁所"的意思。幾天以後，他對我說，很多中國歌迷給他寫信，可他實在太忙，不可能都回信。只有一封信讓他很生氣，所以他才回了信。那個歌迷說："請允許我在您方便的時候與您合影留念。"音樂家回信說："我在方便的時候從來不見客人。"

4. What is true about the musician before he traveled to China?

   (A) He had learned a little Chinese.

   (B) He had learned many languages.

   (C) He had never learned Chinese.

   (D) He had a great interest in learning Chinese.

5. Why did the musician become interested in learning Chinese?

    (A) He thought Chinese was very useful.

    (B) He thought Chinese was pleasant to the ear.

    (C) He had a very good Chinese teacher.

    (D) He had a good Chinese friend.

6. What is the meaning of "方便的时候（方便的時候）" in the Chinese fan's letter?

    (A) When the musician is in the bathroom

    (B) When it is convenient for the musician

    (C) When the musician is taking a photograph

    (D) When the musician is performing

Read this passage.

[Simplified-character version]	[Traditional-character version]
《孙子兵法》是中国现存最早的一部兵书，也是世界上最早的兵书。据说，该书的作者是孙武，人们尊称他为孙子，其中"子"和孔子的"子"读音一样，都是第三声。古代人们用读第三声的"子"来特指有学问的男人，这也是对男人的一种美称。但如果把"子"念成了轻声，那意思就完全不一样了。其实这在汉语中并不少见，汉语中外形相同的汉字往往用不同的读音来表示不同的意义。	《孫子兵法》是中國現存最早的一部兵書，也是世界上最早的兵書。據說，該書的作者是孫武，人們尊稱他爲孫子，其中"子"和孔子的"子"讀音一樣，都是第三聲。古代人們用讀第三聲的"子"來特指有學問的男人，這也是對男人的一種美稱。但如果把"子"念成了輕聲，那意思就完全不一樣了。其實這在漢語中並不少見，漢語中外形相同的漢字往往用不同的讀音來表示不同的意義。

7. What is Sun Tzu's *The Art of War*?

    (A) It talks about the manufacture of weapons.

    (B) It talks about soldiers.

    (C) It talks about Sun Wu.

    (D) It talks about military strategies.

8. In Chinese, the fact that a character may have two different pronunciations is _____ .

    (A) a rare phenomenon

    (B) something that is considered irregular

    (C) something everyone wants to avoid

    (D) a very common phenomenon

9. According to the passage, why should "子（子）" be pronounced in the third tone?

   (A) To show respect to a learned man

   (B) To show love for a grandson

   (C) To show love for a child

   (D) To show respect to a handsome man

Read this e-mail.

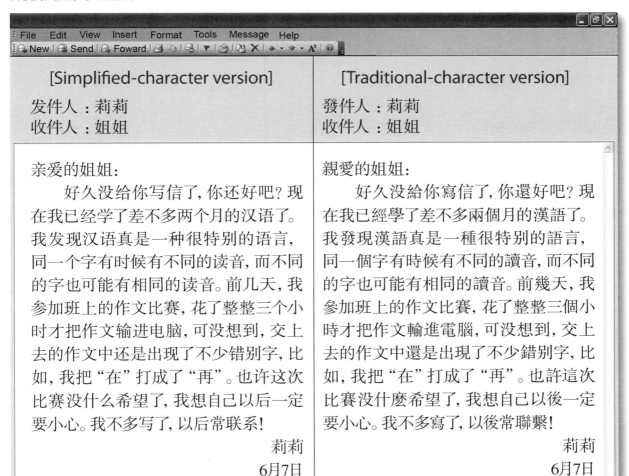

[Simplified-character version]

发件人：莉莉
收件人：姐姐

亲爱的姐姐：

好久没给你写信了，你还好吧？现在我已经学了差不多两个月的汉语了。我发现汉语真是一种很特别的语言，同一个字有时候有不同的读音，而不同的字也可能有相同的读音。前几天，我参加班上的作文比赛，花了整整三个小时才把作文输进电脑，可没想到，交上去的作文中还是出现了不少错别字，比如，我把"在"打成了"再"。也许这次比赛没什么希望了，我想自己以后一定要小心。我不多写了，以后常联系！

莉莉
6月7日

[Traditional-character version]

發件人：莉莉
收件人：姐姐

親愛的姐姐：

好久没給你寫信了，你還好吧？現在我已經學了差不多兩個月的漢語了。我發現漢語真是一種很特別的語言，同一個字有時候有不同的讀音，而不同的字也可能有相同的讀音。前幾天，我參加班上的作文比賽，花了整整三個小時才把作文輸進電腦，可沒想到，交上去的作文中還是出現了不少錯別字，比如，我把"在"打成了"再"。也許這次比賽沒什麼希望了，我想自己以後一定要小心。我不多寫了，以後常聯繫！

莉莉
6月7日

10. What does Li Li say about Chinese?

   (A) It has too many similar-looking characters.

   (B) It is a special language.

   (C) It is not too difficult to learn.

   (D) It has very few words with the same pronunciation.

11. According to the passage, why did Li Li mistype "再（再）" for "在（在）"?

   (A) There was an error with her input method.

   (B) The competition did not allow enough time for checking.

   (C) The two characters have the same pronunciation.

   (D) The two characters are different in appearance.

12. What does Li Li think about the competition?

   (A) She may come in second.

   (B) She may win a prize.

   (C) She may be able to learn a lesson.

   (D) She may not win a prize.

Read this passage.

[Simplified-character version]	[Traditional-character version]
一天麦克在路上碰见了小明。他见小明一副闷闷不乐的样子，就问："你怎么了？""父亲走了。" 小明忍不住哭了起来。麦克觉得很奇怪，就问他："走了？去哪儿了？你怎么这么伤心？"小明回答说："对不起，忘了你是外国人，走了就是去世了的意思。"可是麦克还是不明白去世的意思，但他不敢继续问。回到宿舍后，麦克查了汉语词典，才明白小明家里发生了什么事，也才明白在汉语里"死"字是不能随便用的，尤其是对长辈。	一天麥克在路上碰見了小明。他見小明一副悶悶不樂的樣子，就問："你怎麼了？""父親走了。" 小明忍不住哭了起來。麥克覺得很奇怪，就問他："走了？去哪兒了？你怎麼這麼傷心？"小明回答說："對不起，忘了你是外國人，走了就是去世了的意思。"可是麥克還是不明白去世的意思，但他不敢繼續問。回到宿舍後，麥克查了漢語詞典，才明白小明家裏發生了什麼事，也才明白在漢語裏"死"字是不能隨便用的，尤其是對長輩。

13. According to the passage, why is Xiao Ming unhappy?

   (A) His father has gone to a faraway place.

   (B) His father is away on business.

   (C) His father has passed away.

   (D) His father is injured.

14. How did Mike learn the meaning of "去世（去世）"?

   (A) From his friends

   (B) From his teacher

   (C) From his classmates

   (D) From a reference book

15. According to the passage, why are words like "走（走）" and "去世（去世）" used in place of "死（死）"?

   (A)   The elders prefer to use these expressions.

   (B)   There are many synonyms in Chinese.

   (C)   "死（死）" is an ambiguous term.

   (D)   These expressions show respect to the elders.

Read this passage.

[Simplified-character version]	[Traditional-character version]
在中国，送礼是很有讲究的。有些礼物送给别人，别人一定会很高兴，而有些东西则一定不能随便送人。如果有老人过生日，送桃的话老人一定很高兴，这不是因为老人们喜欢吃桃，而是因为桃象征着长寿，送桃就是祝愿老人长寿，所以给老人送桃又有"送寿桃"这样一种说法。如果送钟的话，那老人就会非常不高兴，因为"钟"和"终"的发音一样，"终"在汉语里是结束的意思，"送终"是送别死去的亲人的意思。	在中國，送禮是很有講究的。有些禮物送給別人，別人一定會很高興，而有些東西則一定不能隨便送人。如果有老人過生日，送桃的話老人一定很高興，這不是因爲老人們喜歡吃桃，而是因爲桃象徵著長壽，送桃就是祝願老人長壽，所以給老人送桃又有"送壽桃"這樣一種說法。如果送鐘的話，那老人就會非常不高興，因爲"鐘"和"終"的發音一樣，"終"在漢語裏是結束的意思，"送終"是送別死去的親人的意思。

16. According to the passage, what must you do when you want to give someone a gift?

   (A)   You should observe certain customs.

   (B)   You can give whatever you want.

   (C)   You can give the person your favorite thing.

   (D)   You had better ask the person what he wants.

17. According to the passage, why are peaches given to the elderly on their birthday?

   (A)   They like to eat peaches.

   (B)   Peaches are nutritious.

   (C)   Peaches symbolize longevity.

   (D)   Peaches symbolize prosperity.

18. Why should a clock NOT be given as a gift?

   (A)   People may associate clocks with "终（終）" which means "the end of life."

   (B)   People may associate it with the passing of time.

   (C)   A clock is not a significant gift.

   (D)   A clock is not very precious.

Read this passage.

[Simplified-character version]	[Traditional-character version]
古时候写东西是没有标点符号的，所以有时同一句话可以有不同的理解。传说有位读书人到朋友家做客，他们聊着聊着，突然下起雨来了。这时天色已晚，于是主人和客人开了个玩笑，他在纸上写了这样一句话："下雨天留客天留人不留"。这句话可以理解为"下雨天留客，天留，人不留！"就是说今天下雨了，老天想把客人留在我家，可是我不想留他在我家。客人笑了笑，拿起笔，在那句话上点了几个标点，句子变成了"下雨天，留客天，留人不?留！"意思是说：下雨天正是应该把客人留下来的天气，究竟要不要留客人住呢? 当然要留! 主人看后，两人一起哈哈大笑起来。	古時候寫東西是没有標點符號的，所以有時同一句話可以有不同的理解。傳説有位讀書人到朋友家做客，他們聊著聊著，突然下起雨來了。這時天色已晚，於是主人和客人開了個玩笑，他在紙上寫了這樣一句話："下雨天留客天留人不留"。這句話可以理解爲"下雨天留客，天留，人不留！"就是説今天下雨了，老天想把客人留在我家，可是我不想留他在我家。客人笑了笑，拿起筆，在那句話上點了幾個標點，句子變成了"下雨天，留客天，留人不?留！"意思是説：下雨天正是應該把客人留下來的天氣，究竟要不要留客人住呢? 當然要留! 主人看後，兩人一起哈哈大笑起來。

19. According to the passage, why did the host NOT punctuate the sentence he had written?

  (A) He had forgotten to add punctuation.

  (B) He wanted to test the scholar.

  (C) He did not know how to punctuate.

  (D) Not punctuating sentences was a standard practice at that time.

20. Why did the host write down the sentence?

  (A) He wanted to keep the scholar at his house.

  (B) He wanted to play a word game with the scholar.

  (C) He wanted to show the scholar his calligraphy skills.

  (D) He wanted to hint to the scholar that he should return home soon.

21. Why did both men laugh?

  (A) They had succeeded in persuading each other.

  (B) They felt embarrassed.

  (C) They thought it was amusing.

  (D) They had the same opinion.

Read this public sign.

[Simplified-character version]

前方施工，车辆绕行

[Traditional-character version]

前方施工，車輛繞行

22. What is the purpose of this sign?

(A) To tell pedestrians to take a different route

(B) To tell people that there is no construction work there

(C) To tell people that there are no motor vehicles there

(D) To tell motorists to take a different route

23. What does "绕行（繞行）" mean?

(A) To make a detour

(B) To drive in circles

(C) To revolve around

(D) To coil around

Read this public sign.

[Simplified-character version]

诚信待客，童叟无欺

[Traditional-character version]

誠信待客，童叟無欺

24. Where would this sign most likely appear?

(A) In a store

(B) In a children's park

(C) In a nursing home

(D) In a reception room

25. What is the purpose of this sign?

(A) To remind people not to cheat others

(B) To tell people that there is no cheating at that place

(C) To remind people to treat customers politely

(D) To let people know that the elderly and the young will receive special assistance

Section Two

I.   Free Response (Writing)

Note: In this part, you may NOT move back and forth among questions.

Directions: You will be asked to write in Chinese in a variety of ways. In each case, you will be asked to write for a specific purpose and to a specific person. You should write in as complete and as culturally appropriate a manner as possible, taking into account the purpose and the person described.

1. Story Narration

The four pictures present a story. Imagine you are writing the story to a friend. Narrate a complete story as suggested by the pictures. Give your story a beginning, a middle, and an end.

2. Personal Letter

Imagine you received a letter from a pen pal. In the letter, he talks about his current life and tells you that he is not happy. Write a reply in letter format. In your letter, tell him what you think about happiness in life and give him some suggestions on how to get rid of his worries.

3. E-Mail Response

Read this e-mail from a friend and then type a response.

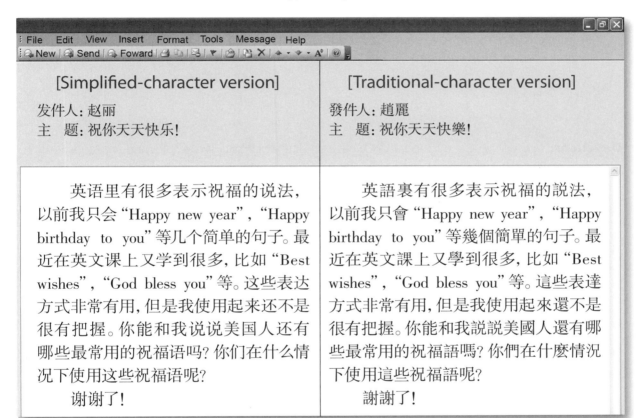

[Simplified-character version]

发件人: 赵丽
主　题: 祝你天天快乐!

　　英语里有很多表示祝福的说法，以前我只会 "Happy new year"，"Happy birthday to you" 等几个简单的句子。最近在英文课上又学到很多，比如 "Best wishes"，"God bless you" 等。这些表达方式非常有用，但是我使用起来还不是很有把握。你能和我说说美国人还有哪些最常用的祝福语吗? 你们在什么情况下使用这些祝福语呢?

　　谢谢了!

[Traditional-character version]

發件人: 趙麗
主　題: 祝你天天快樂!

　　英語裏有很多表示祝福的說法，以前我只會 "Happy new year"，"Happy birthday to you" 等幾個簡單的句子。最近在英文課上又學到很多，比如 "Best wishes"，"God bless you" 等。這些表達方式非常有用，但是我使用起來還不是很有把握。你能和我說說美國人還有哪些最常用的祝福語嗎? 你們在什麼情況下使用這些祝福語呢?

　　謝謝了!

4. Relay a Telephone Message

Imagine you are sharing an apartment with some Chinese friends. You arrive home one day and listen to a message on the answering machine. The message is for one of your housemates. You will listen to the message twice. Then relay the message, including the important details, by typing an e-mail to your friend.

II. Free Response (Speaking)

Note: In this part, you may NOT move back and forth among questions.

Directions: You will participate in a simulated conversation. Each time it is your turn to speak, you will have 20 seconds to record. You should respond as fully and as appropriately as possible.

1. Conversation

The summer vacation is approaching and you are planning to attend summer classes in a language school to improve your knowledge of Chinese. You call the admissions officer and begin a conversation with him.

Directions: You will be asked to speak in Chinese on different topics in the following two questions. In each case, imagine you are making an oral presentation to your class or your family in Chinese. First, you will read and hear the topic for your presentation. You will have 4 minutes to prepare your presentation. Then you will have 2 minutes to record your presentation. Your presentation should be as complete as possible.

2. Cultural Presentation

In your presentation, explain how a Chinese person expresses good wishes on a specific occasion. Good wishes may be expressed through words or by auspicious symbols. You should elaborate on the way these expressions are used and their underlying meanings.

3. Event Plan

Your Chinese teacher has asked you to design an activity plan. The activity is to encourage students to practice their language skills in a Chinese-speaking community. In your presentation, explain the amount of time required for the activity, the venue, and other specific details. You should also emphasize the activity's main segments and point out the advantages and disadvantages of different choices.

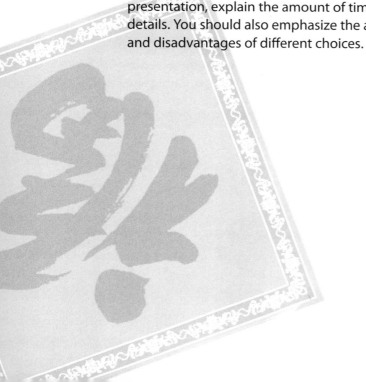

UNIT NINE
LESSON 17 Famous People and History
Who Was Confucius?

Section One

I. Multiple Choice (Listen to the dialogs)

Note: In this part, you may NOT move back and forth among questions.

Directions: In this part, you will hear several short conversations or parts of conversations followed by four choices, designated (A), (B), (C), and (D). Choose the one that continues or completes the conversation in a logical and culturally appropriate manner. You will have 5 seconds to answer each question.

1.	(A)	(B)	(C)	(D)	5.	(A)	(B)	(C)	(D)
2.	(A)	(B)	(C)	(D)	6.	(A)	(B)	(C)	(D)
3.	(A)	(B)	(C)	(D)	7.	(A)	(B)	(C)	(D)
4.	(A)	(B)	(C)	(D)	8.	(A)	(B)	(C)	(D)

II. Multiple Choice (Listen to the selections)

Note: In this part, you may move back and forth only among the questions associated with the current listening selection.

Directions: In this part, you will listen to several selections in Chinese. For each selection, you will be told whether it will be played once or twice. You may take notes as you listen. After listening to each selection, you will see questions in English. For each question, choose the response that is best according to the selection. You will have 12 seconds to answer each question.

Selection 1

1. What does the speaker most likely work as?
    (A) A tour guide
    (B) A curator
    (C) A historian
    (D) A teacher

2. What is the place mentioned in the selection?
   (A) The hometown of Song Qingling
   (B) The place where Song Qingling lived until her death
   (C) The exhibition hall established by Song Qingling
   (D) The house in which Song Qingling's parents lived

3. According to the selection, which of the following statements is TRUE?
   (A) Song Qingling had lived there for more than 60 years.
   (B) The main building of the house has three stories.
   (C) The original decor of the main building has been preserved.
   (D) The date of Song Qingling's death is not mentioned.

Selection 2

4. Who is probably the woman?
   (A) A singer
   (B) A fashion designer
   (C) A movie star
   (D) A soccer star

5. Why did the woman NOT want to have her picture taken with the man?
   (A) They did not know each other.
   (B) The woman was rushing for time.
   (C) The woman did not bring her camera.
   (D) There were too many people around.

6. Where did the man ask the woman to sign her name?
   (A) On a piece of paper
   (B) On his palm
   (C) On his clothes
   (D) On his hat

Selection 3

7. When was this call made?
   (A) In the morning
   (B) At noon
   (C) In the afternoon
   (D) In the evening

8. What kind of association does Wu Li belong to?

   (A) Theater performance   (B) Idiom study

   (C) Film acting   (D) Creative writing

9. What is the main purpose of this call?

   (A) To invite Chen Yan to attend their performance

   (B) To ask Chen Yan when she is available for a discussion

   (C) To ask Chen Yan to choose some idioms for their performance

   (D) To tell Chen Yan that their teacher agrees with their plans

Selection 4

10. According to the talk, what was Sun Yat-sen's father probably working as?

    (A) A doctor   (B) A businessman

    (C) A peasant   (D) A politician

11. What did the young Sun Yat-sen probably major in?

    (A) Education   (B) Political science

    (C) Philosophy   (D) Medicine

12. What is the main focus of this talk?

    (A) It introduces the family of Sun Yat-sen.

    (B) It introduces Sun Yat-sen's life.

    (C) It introduces the revolution of 1911.

    (D) It introduces the academic background of Sun Yat-sen.

Selection 5

13. What is the relationship between the two speakers?

    (A) Brother and sister   (B) Husband and wife

    (C) Friends   (D) Co-workers

14. How many expectant mothers are mentioned in the conversation?

    (A) One   (B) Two

    (C) Three   (D) Four

15. According to the conversation, which of the following statements is TRUE?

    (A) Many people are getting married this year.

    (B) A baby born in the year of the dragon has a promising future.

    (C) The woman is planning to have a baby this year.

    (D) Many people hope that they can have a baby in the year of the dragon.

III. Multiple Choice (Reading)

Note: In this part, you may move back and forth among all the questions.

Directions: You will read several selections in Chinese. Each selection is accompanied by a number of questions in English. For each question, choose the response that is best according to the selection.

Read this e-mail.

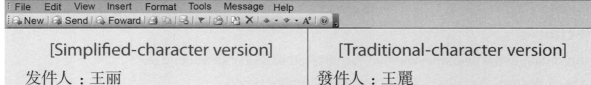

| File | Edit | View | Insert | Format | Tools | Message | Help |

New | Send | Foward

[Simplified-character version]

发件人：王丽
收件人：小明
主　题：最近好吗?

小明:

　　你好!

　　今天我去了大英博物馆。大英博物馆是英国国家博物馆,最早修建于1753年,是一座古罗马立柱式建筑。大英博物馆是全世界收藏东、西方文物最多的博物馆之一,也是收藏中国文物最多的博物馆之一。博物馆共有100多个陈列室,面积六七万平方米,有藏品650多万件。博物馆内设有埃及文物馆、希腊罗马文物馆、西亚文物馆、欧洲中世纪文物馆和东方艺术文物馆。在东方艺术文物馆中,收藏有来自中国、日本、印度和东南亚国家的10多万件文物。其中,中国陈列室就占了好几个大厅,收藏的文物多达23000多件,从殷商钟鼎、周秦器皿、汉唐文物、宋明瓷器到清室宫廷奇珍异宝等等,无所不有。我希望有一天你也能来参观!

王丽

[Traditional-character version]

發件人：王麗
收件人：小明
主　題：最近好嗎?

小明:

　　你好!

　　今天我去了大英博物館。大英博物館是英國國家博物館,最早修建於1753年,是一座古羅馬立柱式建築。大英博物館是全世界收藏東、西方文物最多的博物館之一,也是收藏中國文物最多的博物館之一。博物館共有100多個陳列室,面積六七萬平方米,有藏品650多萬件。博物館內設有埃及文物館、希臘羅馬文物館、西亞文物館、歐洲中世紀文物館和東方藝術文物館。在東方藝術文物館中,收藏有來自中國、日本、印度和東南亞國家的10多萬件文物。其中,中國陳列室就佔了好幾個大廳,收藏的文物多達23000多件,從殷商鐘鼎、周秦器皿、漢唐文物、宋明瓷器到清室宮廷奇珍異寶等等,無所不有。我希望有一天你也能來參觀!

王麗

1. What kind of architectural style does the British Museum have?

   (A) Victorian

   (B) Roman

   (C) Greek

   (D) Gothic

2. Which country's ancient cultural artifacts are NOT mentioned in the e-mail?

   (A) Japan

   (B) India

   (C) Egypt

   (D) Brazil

3. Which of the following statements about the Chinese cultural artifacts exhibited in the British Museum is TRUE?

   (A) They are exhibited in two big exhibition halls.

   (B) There are as many as 30,000 of them.

   (C) Cultural artifacts of the Qing Dynasty imperial family can be found there.

   (D) The exhibition area for Chinese cultural relics covers 60,000 to 70,000 square meters.

Read this weather forecast.

[Simplified-character version]

　　记者从国家气象部门了解到，今年第九号超强台风"圣帕"目前正以每小时二十公里的速度向西北方向移动，预计将于18日凌晨到上午在台湾沿海登陆，登陆后穿过台湾，逐渐向福建海岸靠近，可能于18日夜间到19日上午在福建沿海再次登陆。"圣帕"是今年最强的台风，也是近年来强度最高的台风之一，中心最大风力17级（60米／秒），强度超过去年造成极大危害的"桑美"。

[Traditional-character version]

　　記者從國家氣象部門瞭解到，今年第九號超強颱風"聖帕"目前正以每小時二十公里的速度向西北方向移動，預計將於18日凌晨到上午在臺灣沿海登陸，登陸後穿過臺灣，逐漸向福建海岸靠近，可能於18日夜間到19日上午在福建沿海再次登陸。"聖帕"是今年最強的颱風，也是近年來強度最高的颱風之一，中心最大風力17級（60米／秒），強度超過去年造成極大危害的"桑美"。

4. What does "预计（預計）" mean in the passage?

    (A) To estimate in advance

    (B) To prepare in advance

    (C) To tabulate in advance

    (D) To plan in advance

5. According to the passage, which of the following statements is TRUE?

    (A) Typhoon "圣帕（聖帕）" has landed on the Fujian coast twice.

    (B) The maximum wind of typhoon "桑美（桑美）" reached force 17 near the center.

    (C) Typhoon "圣帕（聖帕）" is moving at a rate of 20 kilometers per hour.

    (D) The residents of the coast of Fujian should be on high alert before dawn on the 18th.

Read this passage.

[Simplified-character version]	[Traditional-character version]
西汉的时候，有个人叫匡衡。他小时候很想读书，可是没钱上学。后来，一个亲戚教他识字，慢慢地，他能看书了。那个时候，书非常贵，于是匡衡就在农忙时节，给有钱的人家打短工，不要工钱，只求人家借书给他看。 　　匡衡长大后，成了家里的主要劳动力。他白天种庄稼，没有时间看书，就只能利用晚上的时间来看书。可是他买不起点灯的油，怎么办呢？ 　　有一天晚上，他看到东边的墙壁上透过来一线亮光。他走到墙壁边一看，原来是邻居的灯光从壁缝里透过来了。于是匡衡想了一个办法：他拿了一把小刀，把墙缝挖大了一些，这样，透过来的光就亮多了，他就凑着透进来的灯光，读起书来。 　　匡衡就是这样刻苦学习，后来成为一个很有学问的人。	西漢的時候，有個人叫匡衡。他小時候很想讀書，可是沒錢上學。後來，一個親戚教他識字，慢慢地，他能看書了。那個時候，書非常貴，於是匡衡就在農忙時節，給有錢的人家打短工，不要工錢，只求人家借書給他看。 　　匡衡長大後，成了家裏的主要勞動力。他白天種莊稼，沒有時間看書，就只能利用晚上的時間來看書。可是他買不起點燈的油，怎麼辦呢？ 　　有一天晚上，他看到東邊的牆壁上透過來一線亮光。他走到牆壁邊一看，原來是鄰居的燈光從壁縫裏透過來了。於是匡衡想了一個辦法：他拿了一把小刀，把牆縫挖大了一些，這樣，透過來的光就亮多了，他就湊著透進來的燈光，讀起書來。 　　匡衡就是這樣刻苦學習，後來成爲一個很有學問的人。

6. Why did Kuang Heng NOT attend school when he was young?

    (A) He was often sick.

    (B) The school was too far away.

    (C) His relatives taught him at home.

    (D) His family was very poor.

7. How did Kuang Heng get books to read?

    (A) He borrowed them from the people he worked for.

    (B) He bought them using the money he earned.

    (C) His relatives gave him books.

    (D) His relatives lent him books.

8. How did Kuang Heng read at night?

    (A) He read in his neighbor's house.

    (B) He borrowed his neighbor's oil lamp.

    (C) He read by the light shining through from his neighbor's house.

    (D) He used an oil lamp purchased with the money he earned.

Read this passage.

[Simplified-character version]	[Traditional-character version]
唐朝著名画家吴道子曾画过一幅孔子像，后来人们只要谈到孔子，脑海中浮现的基本都是吴道子这幅画中孔子的模样。在孔子诞辰2557年纪念日前夕，中国孔子基金会在孔子故里山东曲阜向全球正式发布了一个孔子标准像的定稿。经过修改后的孔子像看上去比原来更加慈祥，眼神也比原来的温和，宽宽的鼻子，大大的嘴，浓浓的眉毛，长长的胡子，是一个具有山东人相貌特征的忠厚长者。然而，并不是所有的人都赞成把孔子的画像标准化。北京东方道德研究所名誉所长、国际儒学联合会理事王殿卿说："我们已经有经过历史检验、被世人普遍认同的吴道子画的孔子像，为什么还要再创造一个标准像去让全世界接受呢？现在的作品能经得起历史检验吗？"	唐朝著名畫家吳道子曾畫過一幅孔子像，後來人們只要談到孔子，腦海中浮現的基本都是吳道子這幅畫中孔子的模樣。在孔子誕辰2557年紀念日前夕，中國孔子基金會在孔子故里山東曲阜向全球正式發佈了一個孔子標準像的定稿。經過修改後的孔子像看上去比原來更加慈祥，眼神也比原來的溫和，寬寬的鼻子，大大的嘴，濃濃的眉毛，長長的鬍子，是一個具有山東人相貌特徵的忠厚長者。然而，並不是所有的人都贊成把孔子的畫像標準化。北京東方道德研究所名譽所長、國際儒學聯合會理事王殿卿說："我們已經有經過歷史檢驗、被世人普遍認同的吳道子畫的孔子像，爲什麼還要再創造一個標準像去讓全世界接受呢？現在的作品能經得起歷史檢驗嗎？"

9. Which of the following descriptions of Confucius are NOT depicted in his new standard portrait?

   (A) Kind, honest, broad nose

   (B) Mild, honest, wide mouth

   (C) Honest, serious, high forehead

   (D) Mild, kind, long beard

10. According to the passage, which of the following statements is TRUE?

   (A) Confucius has been dead for 2,557 years.

   (B) The new standard portrait of Confucius was unveiled by the Confucius Foundation.

   (C) Wu Dao-zi of the Qing Dynasty drew a picture of Confucius.

   (D) The people of Shandong do not like the original portrait.

11. Why do some people disagree with creating a new standard portrait of Confucius?

   (A) There is already a well-recognized portrait of Confucius.

   (B) The portrait drawn by Wu Dao-zi has not endured the test of history.

   (C) The features of Confucius shown in the new portrait are different from the characteristics of the people of Shandong.

   (D) The people in the hometown of Confucius do not agree.

Read this passage.

[Simplified-character version]	[Traditional-character version]
唐朝大诗人李白，小时候不喜欢读书，总觉得书那么多，怎么能读完呢？有一天，李白趁老师不在书房，悄悄地溜出去玩。 他来到山下的小河边，看见一位老婆婆在石头上磨一根很粗的铁棒。李白觉得很奇怪，就上前去问："老婆婆，您磨铁棒做什么？"老婆婆说："我在磨针。"李白吃惊地问："哎呀！铁棒这么粗，针那么细，铁棒怎么能磨成针呢？"老婆婆笑呵呵地说："只要天天磨，每天都不放松，铁棒总能越磨越细，还怕磨不成针吗？"李白听后，心中感到很惭愧，转身跑回了书房。从此，他牢记"只要功夫深，铁棒磨成针"的道理，发奋读书，最后成为一位有名的诗人。	唐朝大詩人李白，小時候不喜歡讀書，總覺得書那麼多，怎麼能讀完呢？有一天，李白趁老師不在書房，悄悄地溜出去玩。 他來到山下的小河邊，看見一位老婆婆在石頭上磨一根很粗的鐵棒。李白覺得很奇怪，就上前去問："老婆婆，您磨鐵棒做什麼？"老婆婆說："我在磨針。"李白吃驚地問："哎呀！鐵棒這麼粗，針那麼細，鐵棒怎麼能磨成針呢？"老婆婆笑呵呵地說："只要天天磨，每天都不放鬆，鐵棒總能越磨越細，還怕磨不成針嗎？"李白聽後，心中感到很慚愧，轉身跑回了書房。從此，他牢記"只要功夫深，鐵棒磨成針"的道理，發奮讀書，最後成爲一位有名的詩人。

12. Why did Li Bai go to the riverside?

   (A) He wanted to meet the elderly woman.

   (B) He sneaked out to avoid reading.

   (C) He wanted to look for his teacher at the riverside.

   (D) He wanted to read at the riverside.

13. What were Li Bai's thoughts after hearing the elderly woman's words?

   (A) He thought the elderly woman had strange ideas.

   (B) He decided he should study hard.

   (C) He decided he wanted to be a great poet.

   (D) He felt he should help the elderly woman.

14. What do the elderly woman's words teach us?

   (A) We cannot have a promising future unless we study hard.

   (B) We will succeed if we have a keen curiosity.

   (C) We can succeed in anything as long as we persevere.

   (D) We should learn with a glad heart.

Read this passage.

[Simplified-character version]	[Traditional-character version]
那天在课上，老师问我们以后想做什么，我们说出了各自的想法。老师说，如果我们生活在古代的中国，一定都想成为一个读书人，因为在那时只有读书人才会受到人们的尊重，也往往会有更多的机会，比如通过考试成为一名官员。中国两千多年来一直都认为读书人的地位是最高的，其次是从事农业生产的人，再次是手工业者，地位最低的是商人。所以俗话说，"万般皆下品，唯有读书高"。现在人们的观念跟以前可不一样了，比如商人的地位就提高了，许多人想经商，做一个有钱人。	那天在課上，老師問我們以後想做什麼，我們說出了各自的想法。老師說，如果我們生活在古代的中國，一定都想成為一個讀書人，因為在那時只有讀書人才會受到人們的尊重，也往往會有更多的機會，比如通過考試成為一名官員。中國兩千多年來一直都認為讀書人的地位是最高的，其次是從事農業生產的人，再次是手工業者，地位最低的是商人。所以俗話說，"萬般皆下品，唯有讀書高"。現在人們的觀念跟以前可不一樣了，比如商人的地位就提高了，許多人想經商，做一個有錢人。

15. According to the passage, what is the order of the social class structure in ancient China in descending order?

   (A) Scholars, merchants, farmers, craftsmen

   (B) Scholars, farmers, merchants, craftsmen

   (C) Scholars, merchants, craftsmen, farmers

   (D) Scholars, farmers, craftsmen, merchants

16. Why did people want to be scholars in ancient China?

   (A) They had more opportunities.

   (B) They earned the most money.

   (C) They could live a carefree life.

   (D) They did not have to pay taxes.

17. What does "万般皆下品，唯有读书高（萬般皆下品，唯有讀書高）" mean?

   (A) Studying is most important.

   (B) Scholars enjoy the highest position in society.

   (C) Studying demands the greatest amount of effort.

   (D) Scholars have the finest taste.

18. According to the passage, which of the following statements is TRUE?

   (A) Farmers enjoy a higher status now compared to the past.

   (B) Craftsmen enjoy a higher status now compared to the past.

   (C) Merchants enjoy a higher status now compared to the past.

   (D) Scholars enjoy a higher status now compared to the past.

Read this passage.

[Simplified-character version]	[Traditional-character version]
2000多年以前的春秋时期，中国由几十个大大小小的诸侯国组成，他们为了争夺土地，经常进行战争。经过多年的战争，许多小诸侯国被消灭了，到了战国时期，只剩下十几个诸侯国，而其中最具影响力的有七个，又称"战国七雄"。这七个诸侯国控制了中国大部分土地，他们为了各自的利益，时而合作，时而开战，直到公元前221年，秦始皇统一了六国，战国时代才结束。虽然春秋、战国时代的政治很混乱，但那时的思想文化却十分繁荣，出现了很多著名的思想家和不同的学术流派，像老子、庄子、孔子、孟子等人的思想都是在那个时代产生的。	2000多年以前的春秋時期，中國由幾十個大大小小的諸侯國組成，他們爲了爭奪土地，經常進行戰爭。經過多年的戰爭，許多小諸侯國被消滅了，到了戰國時期，只剩下十幾個諸侯國，而其中最具影響力的有七個，又稱"戰國七雄"。這七個諸侯國控制了中國大部分土地，他們爲了各自的利益，時而合作，時而開戰，直到公元前221年，秦始皇統一了六國，戰國時代才結束。雖然春秋、戰國時代的政治很混亂，但那時的思想文化卻十分繁榮，出現了很多著名的思想家和不同的學術流派，像老子、莊子、孔子、孟子等人的思想都是在那個時代產生的。

19. What does "战国七雄（戰國七雄）" refer to in the passage?
    (A) The seven princedoms that existed during the Warring States Period
    (B) The different academic schools of thought that evolved in the seven princedoms during the Warring States Period
    (C) The seven famous heroes of the Warring States Period
    (D) The seven princedoms that had the greatest power and influence during the Warring States Period

20. What are the distinguishing characteristics of the Spring and Autumn Period?
    (A) A united nation and a prosperous society
    (B) Advanced philosophy and culture
    (C) Many political parties
    (D) Many academic schools of thought

21. According to the passage, which of the following statements is TRUE?
    (A) During the reign of Qin Shi Huang, China was made up of seven princedoms.
    (B) During the Spring and Autumn Period, China was made up of scores of princedoms.
    (C) The Warring States Period lasted until 221 A.D.
    (D) Lao Zi and Zhuang Zi both lived during the reign of Qin Shi Huang.

Read this public sign.

[Simplified-character version] [Traditional-character version]

严禁攀爬 嚴禁攀爬

22. Where would this sign most likely appear?

   (A) On slides at a playground

   (B) At an accident site

   (C) On a high-voltage telegraph pole

   (D) Outside an office building

23. What is the purpose of this sign?

   (A) To warn people not to climb

   (B) To warn people not to trespass

   (C) To remind people that the road is blocked

   (D) To remind people that the road is only for special use

Read this public sign.

[Simplified-character version] [Traditional-character version]

小件行李寄存处 小件行李寄存處

24. Where would this sign most likely appear?

   (A) In a museum

   (B) In a library

   (C) In a post office

   (D) In a railway station

25. Which of the following statements about the sign is TRUE?

   (A) People can mail parcels there.

   (B) People can mail luggage there.

   (C) People can store schoolbags there.

   (D) People can store luggage there.

Section Two

I. Free Response (Writing)

Note: In this part, you may NOT move back and forth among questions.

Directions: You will be asked to write in Chinese in a variety of ways. In each case, you will be asked to write for a specific purpose and to a specific person. You should write in as complete and as culturally appropriate a manner as possible, taking into account the purpose and the person described.

1. Story Narration

The four pictures present a story. Imagine you are writing the story to a friend. Narrate a complete story as suggested by the pictures. Give your story a beginning, a middle, and an end.

2. Personal Letter

Imagine you received a letter from a pen pal. In the letter, he talks about his aspirations in life. He says Bill Gates has influenced him a great deal, and that as a result, he wants to major in computer science when he goes to college. Write a reply in letter format. Tell your pen pal about your plans for the future, and tell him why you made such plans.

3. E-Mail Response

Read this e-mail from a friend and then type a response.

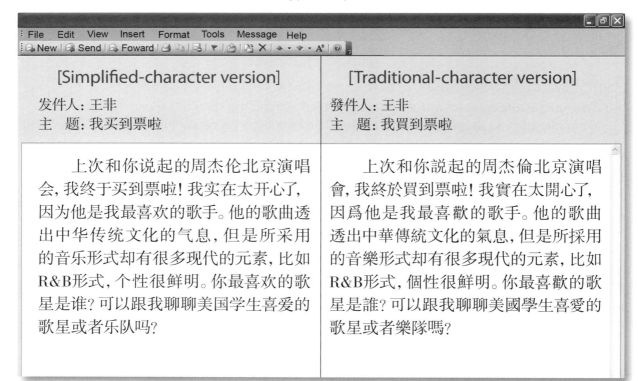

File Edit View Insert Format Tools Message Help	
New Send Foward	
[Simplified-character version]	[Traditional-character version]
发件人: 王非 主　题: 我买到票啦	發件人: 王非 主　題: 我買到票啦
上次和你说起的周杰伦北京演唱会, 我终于买到票啦! 我实在太开心了, 因为他是我最喜欢的歌手。他的歌曲透出中华传统文化的气息, 但是所采用的音乐形式却有很多现代的元素, 比如R&B形式, 个性很鲜明。你最喜欢的歌星是谁? 可以跟我聊聊美国学生喜爱的歌星或者乐队吗?	上次和你説起的周杰倫北京演唱會, 我終於買到票啦! 我實在太開心了, 因爲他是我最喜歡的歌手。他的歌曲透出中華傳統文化的氣息, 但是所採用的音樂形式卻有很多現代的元素, 比如R&B形式, 個性很鮮明。你最喜歡的歌星是誰? 可以跟我聊聊美國學生喜愛的歌星或者樂隊嗎?

4. Relay a Telephone Message

Imagine you are sharing an apartment with some Chinese friends. You arrive home one day and listen to a message on the answering machine. The message is for one of your housemates. You will listen twice to the message. Then relay the message, including the important details, by typing an e-mail to your friend.

II. Free Response (Speaking)

Note: In this part, you may NOT move back and forth among questions.

Directions: You will participate in a simulated conversation. Each time it is your turn to speak, you will have 20 seconds to record. You should respond as fully and as appropriately as possible.

1. Conversation

Your vacation has begun. You have left the United States and are traveling to China. On the plane, you chat with the passenger sitting beside you.

Directions: You will be asked to speak in Chinese on different topics in the following two questions. In each case, imagine you are making an oral presentation to your class or your family in Chinese. First, you will read and hear the topic for your presentation. You will have 4 minutes to prepare your presentation. Then you will have 2 minutes to record your presentation. Your presentation should be as complete as possible.

2. Cultural Presentation

Choose ONE famous Chinese historical or cultural figure whose life you are familiar with. In your presentation, describe clearly this person's life and influence.

3. Event Plan

Your school has decided to hold an exhibition showcasing its history and alumni celebrities. You are in charge of organizing this event. In your presentation, briefly introduce the reason for this exhibition. You should also explain clearly how the exhibition will be presented and work out all the needs and requirements, such as getting students' collaboration.

UNIT NINE Famous People and History
LESSON 18 China Highlights

Section One

I. Multiple Choice (Listen to the dialogs)

Note: In this part, you may NOT move back and forth among questions.

Directions: In this part, you will hear several short conversations or parts of conversations followed by four choices, designated (A), (B), (C), and (D). Choose the one that continues or completes the conversation in a logical and culturally appropriate manner. You will have 5 seconds to answer each question.

1.	(A)	(B)	(C)	(D)	5.	(A)	(B)	(C)	(D)
2.	(A)	(B)	(C)	(D)	6.	(A)	(B)	(C)	(D)
3.	(A)	(B)	(C)	(D)	7.	(A)	(B)	(C)	(D)
4.	(A)	(B)	(C)	(D)	8.	(A)	(B)	(C)	(D)

II. Multiple Choice (Listen to the selections)

Note: In this part, you may move back and forth only among the questions associated with the current listening selection.

Directions: In this part, you will listen to several selections in Chinese. For each selection, you will be told whether it will be played once or twice. You may take notes as you listen. After listening to each selection, you will see questions in English. For each question, choose the response that is best according to the selection. You will have 12 seconds to answer each question.

Selection 1

1. Why are the houses on both sides of the street being repaired?
    (A) They are no longer popular.
    (B) They affect the city's image.
    (C) They are worn out.
    (D) They have new owners.

2. According to the conversation, how old are the houses?
   (A) About 30 years old
   (B) About 100 years old
   (C) About 130 years old
   (D) About 150 years old

3. According to the conversation, which of the following statements is TRUE?
   (A) The man thinks it is easy to preserve houses with wooden structures.
   (B) The woman thinks it is difficult to preserve houses with wooden structures.
   (C) The houses with wooden structures are poor in quality.
   (D) The houses on both sides of the street often get repaired.

4. What does "谁都知道（誰都知道）" mean in the conversation?
   (A) The woman does not know who knows.
   (B) The woman asks the man who knows.
   (C) The woman knows now.
   (D) The woman thinks everyone knows.

Selection 2

5. Why does the speaker suggest going to the Simatai Great Wall?
   (A) It is the oldest part of the ancient Great Wall.
   (B) It has just been restored.
   (C) It was developed a long time ago as a scenic spot.
   (D) It has retained the original features of the Ming Dynasty Great Wall.

6. According to the voice message, which of the following statements is TRUE?
   (A) Wang Lan knows a lot about the Simatai Great Wall.
   (B) Xiao Tian went to the Simatai Great Wall with her friends last weekend.
   (C) The Simatai Great Wall has been fully commercialized.
   (D) The Simatai Great Wall is not as steep compared to the other parts of the Great Wall.

Selection 3

7. How does the woman feel about the man going to Xi'an over the weekend?
   (A) Angry
   (B) Happy
   (C) Surprised
   (D) Envious

8. What did the man mean by "难道我还骗你（難道我還騙你）"?

   (A) He wanted to cheat her.

   (B) It was hard for him to cheat her.

   (C) He did not mean to cheat her.

   (D) He did not cheat her.

9. According to the conversation, why did the man go to Xi'an?

   (A) An express train goes there.

   (B) He wanted to buy some souvenirs.

   (C) Xi'an is a well-known ancient capital.

   (D) Xi'an is not very far away.

10. What did the man want to express when he said "这是我的一点心意（這是我的一點心意）"?

    (A) His gratitude

    (B) His friendship

    (C) His regret

    (D) His apology

Selection 4

11. Which of the following statements about the natural disaster is TRUE?

    (A) The hurricane affected the eastern part of China.

    (B) The hurricane happened a few days ago.

    (C) More than 1,000 people died in the hurricane.

    (D) About 200 people were left homeless after the hurricane.

12. What can the students donate to help the people affected by the hurricane?

    (A) Money and clothes

    (B) Food and medicine

    (C) Books and stationery

    (D) Tents and blankets

13. What is the purpose of this talk?

    (A) To reiterate the news about the hurricane

    (B) To report on the damage caused by the hurricane

    (C) To explain the reasons for the disaster

    (D) To call on the students to help the disaster-stricken people

Selection 5

14. What did the woman do earlier?

(A) She learned calligraphy.

(B) She did some research on ancient writing materials.

(C) She practiced calligraphy.

(D) She saw the ancient writing materials.

15. According to the conversation, what contribution was made by Cai Lun?

(A) He created characters by casting them on a metal apparatus.

(B) He created characters by engraving them on animal stones.

(C) He improved the technique of making paper.

(D) He improved the technique of writing.

III. Multiple Choice (Reading)

Note: In this part, you may move back and forth among all the questions.

Directions: You will read several selections in Chinese. Each selection is accompanied by a number of questions in English. For each question, choose the response that is best according to the selection.

Read this passage.

[Simplified-character version]	[Traditional-character version]
中国是世界上最早发现茶树叶的功用，并加以利用的国家。据说，最早发现茶和利用茶的人是神农。传说他为了找到能治病的植物，曾经亲自尝遍百草。他在一次误吃了有毒的草以后，又吃了几片茶树叶，发现茶叶可以用来解毒。因此，在最初很长的一段时间里，茶叶一直被当作药物来使用。直到秦、汉时期，人们发现茶叶泡的水有让人头脑清醒的功效，茶才逐渐成为一种饮料，人工种植的茶树也多了起来，制茶和饮茶渐成风气。	中國是世界上最早發現茶樹葉的功用，並加以利用的國家。據説，最早發現茶和利用茶的人是神農。傳説他爲了找到能治病的植物，曾經親自嚐遍百草。他在一次誤吃了有毒的草以後，又吃了幾片茶樹葉，發現茶葉可以用來解毒。因此，在最初很長的一段時間裏，茶葉一直被當作藥物來使用。直到秦、漢時期，人們發現茶葉泡的水有讓人頭腦清醒的功效，茶才逐漸成爲一種飲料，人工種植的茶樹也多了起來，製茶和飲茶漸成風氣。

1. According to the passage, how were tea leaves used in the beginning?

   (A) As food

   (B) As luxury goods

   (C) As beverages

   (D) As medicine

2. According to the passage, which of the following statements is TRUE?

   (A) Shennong discovered that tea has restorative properties.

   (B) Tea plants were widely planted before the Qing and Han Dynasty.

   (C) Some tea leaves are poisonous.

   (D) Tea leaves have been used by the Chinese since the early days.

3. What does "渐成风气（漸成風氣）" mean here?

   (A) To become a wisp of air

   (B) To become a waft of wind

   (C) To become increasingly popular

   (D) To become increasingly numerous

Read this passage.

[Simplified-character version]	[Traditional-character version]
有一句俗话叫"乱世出英雄"，意思是说在很混乱的年代往往会有英雄出现。其实不光是"乱世出英雄"，"乱世"还出美女呢! 中国古代最有名的四大美女, 其中的三位所生活的年代就不是很太平, 而且据说也正是因为这些美女与当时的政治有很大的关系, 她们在中国历史上才更加有名。就说四大美女中的王昭君吧, 她长得非常漂亮, 后来嫁给了北方的一个少数民族部落首领, 自那以后, 中原地区很长一段时间没有再发生战争。	有一句俗話叫"亂世出英雄"，意思是說在很混亂的年代往往會有英雄出現。其實不光是"亂世出英雄"，"亂世"還出美女呢! 中國古代最有名的四大美女, 其中的三位所生活的年代就不是很太平, 而且據說也正是因爲這些美女與當時的政治有很大的關係, 她們在中國歷史上才更加有名。就說四大美女中的王昭君吧, 她長得非常漂亮, 後來嫁給了北方的一個少數民族部落首領, 自那以後, 中原地區很長一段時間沒有再發生戰爭。

4. What does "乱世（亂世）" mean in the passage?

   (A) Things that are tumultuous

   (B) A tumultuous society

   (C) An attempt to create a chaotic world

   (D) An attempt to be heroic in chaotic times

5. According to the passage, why were the four great beauties of ancient China famous in Chinese history?

(A) They were very beautiful.

(B) They were beautiful and smart.

(C) They lived in tumultuous times.

(D) They had some bearing on the political situation.

6. Wang Zhaojun, one of the four great beauties of ancient China, _____ .

(A) was married to a tribal chief in Central China

(B) brought peace to Central China

(C) lived in a peace era

(D) was married to a hero

Read this passage.

[Simplified-character version]	[Traditional-character version]
晋代的祖逖小时候是个不爱读书的孩子，长大以后，他认识到不读书就不能为国家贡献力量，于是就发奋读起书来。经过了几年的刻苦学习，他的学问大有长进。 后来，祖逖和他小时候的好友刘琨一起做官。有一次，半夜里祖逖被公鸡的叫声惊醒了。这时，四周还一片漆黑，他把刘琨叫起来，对他说：“你听，鸡叫了，咱们起床练剑怎么样？”刘琨很高兴地同意了。从此以后，他们每天听到鸡叫就起床练剑，一年四季从不间断。功夫不负有心人，经过长期的刻苦学习和训练，他们终于成为能文能武的全才，既能写得一手好文章，又能带兵打胜仗，为国家做出了很大贡献。这个故事就是成语“闻鸡起舞”的由来。	晉代的祖逖小時候是個不愛讀書的孩子，長大以後，他認識到不讀書就不能爲國家貢獻力量，於是就發奮讀起書來。經過了幾年的刻苦學習，他的學問大有長進。 後來，祖逖和他小時候的好友劉琨一起做官。有一次，半夜裏祖逖被公鷄的叫聲驚醒了。這時，四週還一片漆黑，他把劉琨叫起來，對他説：“你聽，鷄叫了，咱們起床練劍怎麼樣？”劉琨很高興地同意了。從此以後，他們每天聽到鷄叫就起床練劍，一年四季從不間斷。功夫不負有心人，經過長期的刻苦學習和訓練，他們終於成爲能文能武的全才，既能寫得一手好文章，又能帶兵打勝仗，爲國家做出了很大貢獻。這個故事就是成語“聞鷄起舞”的由來。

7. Which of the following statements about Zu Ti and Liu Kun is TRUE?

(A) They both loved studying even as young children.

(B) They practiced sword together for a year.

(C) They studied together every evening.

(D) They have been good friends since childhood.

8. What does "功夫不负有心人（功夫不負有心人）" mean in the passage?

   (A) You will be able to reap rewards as long as you put in efforts.

   (B) You will be an observant person as long as you pay attention to things around you.

   (C) You will be able to serve your nation as long as you practice martial arts.

   (D) You will be able to survive in society as long as you have good martial arts skills.

9. What does "闻鸡起舞（聞鷄起舞）" mean here?

   (A) Getting up to practice dancing upon hearing the cock's crowing

   (B) Getting up to practice sword upon hearing the cock's crowing

   (C) Dancing with joy upon hearing the cock's crowing

   (D) Being woken abruptly upon hearing the cock's crowing

Read this passage.

[Simplified-character version]	[Traditional-character version]
有一个男孩脾气很坏，于是父亲就给了他一袋钉子，并且告诉他，发脾气的时候就在木头上钉一根钉子。第一天，这个男孩钉下了37根钉子。渐渐地，男孩每天钉下钉子的数量减少了。 　　男孩慢慢地发现，控制自己的脾气要比钉下那些钉子容易些。终于有一天，这个男孩再也不乱发脾气了，他把这些告诉了他的父亲。父亲对他说，从现在开始，每当他能控制自己的脾气的时候，就拔出一根钉子。 　　一天天过去了，男孩终于拔出了所有的钉子。父亲握着他的手说："你做得很好，我的孩子，但是你看看木头上的那些洞。它们永远不能恢复到从前的样子了。"	有一個男孩脾氣很壞，於是父親就給了他一袋釘子，並且告訴他，發脾氣的時候就在木頭上釘一根釘子。第一天，這個男孩釘下了37根釘子。漸漸地，男孩每天釘下釘子的數量減少了。 　　男孩慢慢地發現，控制自己的脾氣要比釘下那些釘子容易些。終於有一天，這個男孩再也不亂發脾氣了，他把這些告訴了他的父親。父親對他說，從現在開始，每當他能控制自己的脾氣的時候，就拔出一根釘子。 　　一天天過去了，男孩終於拔出了所有的釘子。父親握著他的手說："你做得很好，我的孩子，但是你看看木頭上的那些洞。它們永遠不能恢復到從前的樣子了。"

10. Why did the number of nails knocked in by the boy become fewer and fewer?

   (A) The nails in the package became fewer and fewer.

   (B) The number of times the boy got angry became fewer and fewer.

   (C) The pieces of wood where the nail could be knocked in got fewer and fewer.

   (D) His interest in this game became less and less.

11. According to the passage, which of the following statements is TRUE?

(A) The boy's temper got from bad to worse.

(B) The father gave his son some nails to learn some carpentry work.

(C) The boy knocked the nails into the wood in order to vent his anger.

(D) The boy discovered that it was much harder to knock in a nail than to hold his temper.

12. What does "它们永远不能恢复到从前的样子了（它們永遠不能恢復到從前的樣子了）" mean?

(A) The consequences of a mistake are hard to undo.

(B) One should correct his mistake as soon as he realizes it.

(C) It is hard to change one's personality.

(D) It is hard to keep calm when one is angry.

Read this passage.

[Simplified-character version]	[Traditional-character version]
安妮在二手市场买了一台笔记本电脑，使用不到三个月，电脑经常无缘无故地死机。她把电脑拿到一家修理店，老板开价600元。安妮觉得太贵，转到另一家修理店。这家店的老板说，电脑要彻底杀毒，需要100元。安妮想了想，说："我出来匆忙，忘记带钱了，明天再来吧。"接着，她又换了一家维修店，只见老板打开电脑机壳看了看，说："好修，10元钱。"说着便拿起烙铁，毫不犹豫地在里面点了一下。安妮一试，电脑再也打不开了。安妮非常着急，大声问："以前我的电脑只是经常死机，还可以用，怎么你一修，都没法启动了？"老板听后大惊，说："什么？电脑？我还以为是新式收音机呢。你怎么不早说？"安妮抬头一看门前的招牌，才发现上面写的是："修理各类收音机"。	安妮在二手市場買了一臺筆記本電腦，使用不到三個月，電腦經常無緣無故地死機。她把電腦拿到一家修理店，老板開價600元。安妮覺得太貴，轉到另一家修理店。這家店的老板說，電腦要徹底殺毒，需要100元。安妮想了想，說："我出來匆忙，忘記帶錢了，明天再來吧。"接着，她又換了一家維修店，只見老板打開電腦機殼看了看，說："好修，10元錢。"說着便拿起烙鐵，毫不猶豫地在裏面點了一下。安妮一試，電腦再也打不開了。安妮非常著急，大聲問："以前我的電腦只是經常死機，還可以用，怎麼你一修，都没法啓動了？"老板聽後大驚，說："什麼？電腦？我還以爲是新式收音機呢。你怎麼不早說？"安妮抬頭一看門前的招牌，才發現上面寫的是："修理各類收音機"。

13. Which of the following most likely did NOT cause Annie's computer to break down?

    (A) Annie did not use it properly.

    (B) Her computer was infected with a virus.

    (C) Annie broke it by accident.

    (D) The computer was probably too old.

14. Why did Annie leave the second repair shop?

    (A) She wanted to find a shop which would charge a lower fee.

    (B) The shop owner was impolite.

    (C) She forgot to bring money with her.

    (D) The shop charged a higher fee than the first one.

15. Why did the third shop charge so little?

    (A) The shop was having a promotion.

    (B) The computer was easy to fix.

    (C) The shop owner thought it was a radio.

    (D) The shop was at an unfavorable location.

Read this passage.

[Simplified-character version]	[Traditional-character version]
一只老虎抓住了一只狐狸。就在老虎准备饱餐一顿的时候，狐狸对老虎说："我是天帝派到山林中来当百兽之王的，你要是吃了我，天帝是不会饶恕你的。"老虎对狐狸的话半信半疑，便问："你是百兽之王，有什么证据？"狐狸赶紧说："你如果不相信，可以跟我到山林中去走一走。"老虎觉得这也是个办法，于是就让狐狸在前面带路，自己跟在后面，一起向山林的深处走去。山林中的野兽远远地看见它们，一个个都吓得魂飞魄散，纷纷逃跑。狐狸洋洋得意地对老虎说道："现在你看到了吧？山林中的野兽，有谁敢不怕我？"于是老虎放了狐狸。	一隻老虎抓住了一隻狐狸。就在老虎準備飽餐一頓的時候，狐狸對老虎説："我是天帝派到山林中來當百獸之王的，你要是吃了我，天帝是不會饒恕你的。"老虎對狐狸的話半信半疑，便問："你是百獸之王，有什麼證據？"狐狸趕緊説："你如果不相信，可以跟我到山林中去走一走。"老虎覺得這也是個辦法，於是就讓狐狸在前面帶路，自己跟在後面，一起向山林的深處走去。山林中的野獸遠遠地看見牠們，一個個都嚇得魂飛魄散，紛紛逃跑。狐狸洋洋得意地對老虎説道："現在你看到了吧？山林中的野獸，有誰敢不怕我？"於是老虎放了狐狸。

16. Why did the tiger NOT immediately devour the fox after catching it?

    (A) The tiger was not hungry.

    (B) The fox said he was sent to earth by God.

    (C) The fox said he could work as the tiger's guide.

    (D) The tiger thought the fox was very pitiful.

17. What does "半信半疑（半信半疑）" mean in the passage?

    (A) One is not sure about something.

    (B) One neither believes nor doubts something.

    (C) One seems to believe something, but he doubts it in fact.

    (D) One seems to doubt something, but he believes it in fact.

18. How did the fox scare away all the animals?

    (A) By taking advantage of the tiger's prestige

    (B) By citing the name of God

    (C) By using his own power

    (D) By depending on the help of his friends

Read this passage.

[Simplified-character version]	[Traditional-character version]
在中国，以前城里人的住房一般是由单位分配的，不需要购买，只需要付很少的房租，但是选择的余地也很小。单位的房子在哪儿，你就得住哪儿；单位的房子什么样，你就得住什么样的房子。现在，单位不管个人的房子了，每个人都得自己买房子。市场上有各种各样的商品房，这些房子所处地区不同，环境不同，建筑的标准也不相同，因此在价格上有很大差异。如果你有钱，你就可以买到各方面都满意的房子；可是对于收入低的人来说，买什么样的房子就是一个很让人头疼的问题了。	在中國，以前城裏人的住房一般是由單位分配的，不需要購買，只需要付很少的房租，但是選擇的餘地也很小。單位的房子在哪兒，你就得住哪兒；單位的房子什麼樣，你就得住什麼樣的房子。現在，單位不管個人的房子了，每個人都得自己買房子。市場上有各種各樣的商品房，這些房子所處地區不同，環境不同，建築的標準也不相同，因此在價格上有很大差異。如果你有錢，你就可以買到各方面都滿意的房子；可是對於收入低的人來說，買什麼樣的房子就是一個很讓人頭疼的問題了。

19. According to the passage, how were the houses of city dwellers like in the past?

    (A) There were a wide selection to choose from.

    (B) They were bought by themselves.

    (C) They were provided by their respective units.

    (D) There were many satisfactory features.

20. What does "管（管）" in "单位不管个人的房子了（單位不管個人的房子了）" mean in the passage?

   (A) Manage
   (B) Provide
   (C) Operate
   (D) Guarantee

21. According to the passage, which of the following statements is TRUE?

   (A) Most of the city dwellers have to purchase a house by themselves now.
   (B) People with lower incomes can only buy houses in the suburbs.
   (C) One does not have to pay rent for the houses provided by the unit.
   (D) The construction standards of all commercial housing are very high.

Read this public sign.

[Simplified-character version]

施工带来不便，敬请谅解

[Traditional-character version]

施工帶來不便，敬請諒解

22. Where would this sign most likely appear?

   (A) On a bus
   (B) At a construction site
   (C) On a billboard
   (D) In a classroom

23. What is the purpose of this sign?

   (A) To express one's apology
   (B) To warn somebody
   (C) To show one's respect
   (D) To show one's understanding

Read this public sign.

[Simplified-character version]

置于阴凉干燥处

[Traditional-character version]

置於陰涼乾燥處

24. Where would this sign most likely appear?

   (A) On a cupboard
   (B) On children's toys
   (C) On a book cover
   (D) On a food package

25. What is the purpose of this sign?

   (A) To tell people how to preserve something
   (B) To tell people how to pick a position
   (C) To remind people to be careful when carrying the item
   (D) To remind people to keep the place cool and dry

Section Two

I. Free Response (Writing)

Note: In this part, you may NOT move back and forth among questions.

Directions: You will be asked to write in Chinese in a variety of ways. In each case, you will be asked to write for a specific purpose and to a specific person. You should write in as complete and as culturally appropriate a manner as possible, taking into account the purpose and the person described.

1. Story Narration

The four pictures present a story. Imagine you are writing the story to a friend. Narrate a complete story as suggested by the pictures. Give your story a beginning, a middle, and an end.

2. Personal Letter

Imagine you received a letter from a pen pal. In the letter, he says that learning English has been like opening a window for him, through which he can enjoy a colorful English world. He also asks about your study of the Chinese language and what you think of it. Write a reply in letter format. Tell you pen pal what you think about the relationship between learning the Chinese language and understanding Chinese culture.

3. E-Mail Response

Read this e-mail from a friend and then type a response.

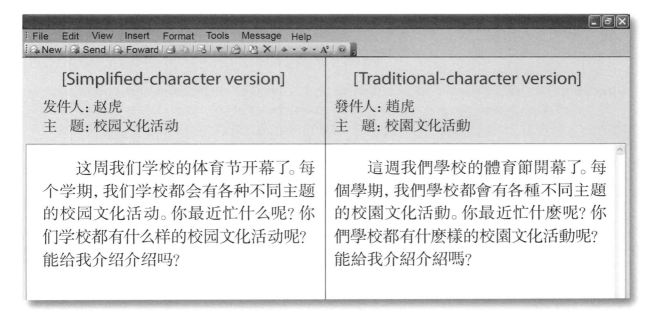

File   Edit   View   Insert   Format   Tools   Message   Help
New | Send | Foward |

[Simplified-character version]	[Traditional-character version]
发件人: 赵虎 主　题: 校园文化活动	發件人: 趙虎 主　题: 校園文化活動
这周我们学校的体育节开幕了。每个学期，我们学校都会有各种不同主题的校园文化活动。你最近忙什么呢? 你们学校都有什么样的校园文化活动呢? 能给我介绍介绍吗?	這週我們學校的體育節開幕了。每個學期，我們學校都會有各種不同主題的校園文化活動。你最近忙什麼呢? 你們學校都有什麼樣的校園文化活動呢? 能給我介紹介紹嗎?

4. Relay a Telephone Message

Imagine you are sharing an apartment with some Chinese friends. You arrive home one day and listen to a message on the answering machine. The message is for one of your housemates. You will listen twice to the message. Then relay the message, including the important details, by typing an e-mail to your friend.

II. Free Response (Speaking)

Note: In this part, you may NOT move back and forth among questions.

Directions: You will participate in a simulated conversation. Each time it is your turn to speak, you will have 20 seconds to record. You should respond as fully and as appropriately as possible.

1. Conversation

Recently you have learnt a lot about Chinese history and have come to know of many Chinese stories, both inside and outside the classroom. You chat with your Chinese cyber friend about a history topic.

Directions: You will be asked to speak in Chinese on different topics in the following two questions. In each case, imagine you are making an oral presentation to your class or your family in Chinese. First, you will read and hear the topic for your presentation. You will have 4 minutes to prepare your presentation. Then you will have 2 minutes to record your presentation. Your presentation should be as complete as possible.

2. Cultural Presentation

"Respecting the old and loving the young" is regarded as a traditional virtue in China. In your presentation, talk about your understanding of such family relationships. You should also describe the main manifestations of such relationships and the cultural concepts related to them.

3. Event Plan

You are planning to launch your Chinese blog. In your presentation, explain why you want to start such a blog. You may also describe how you will design the webpage or how you intend to let your friends know about your blog, etc.

UNIT TEN
LESSON 19 Literature and Arts
"To Borrow Arrows with Thatched Boats"

Section One

I. Multiple Choice (Listen to the dialogs)

Note: In this part, you may NOT move back and forth among questions.

Directions: In this part, you will hear several short conversations or parts of conversations followed by four choices, designated (A), (B), (C), and (D). Choose the one that continues or completes the conversation in a logical and culturally appropriate manner. You will have 5 seconds to answer each question.

1.	(A)	(B)	(C)	(D)	5.	(A)	(B)	(C)	(D)
2.	(A)	(B)	(C)	(D)	6.	(A)	(B)	(C)	(D)
3.	(A)	(B)	(C)	(D)	7.	(A)	(B)	(C)	(D)
4.	(A)	(B)	(C)	(D)	8.	(A)	(B)	(C)	(D)

II. Multiple Choice (Listen to the selections)

Note: In this part, you may move back and forth only among the questions associated with the current listening selection.

Directions: In this part, you will listen to several selections in Chinese. For each selection, you will be told whether it will be played once or twice. You may take notes as you listen. After listening to each selection, you will see questions in English. For each question, choose the response that is best according to the selection. You will have 12 seconds to answer each question.

Selection 1

1. Where is the "风采展（風采展）" located?
   (A) On the first floor
   (B) On the second floor
   (C) On the third floor
   (D) On the fourth floor

2. Which of the following is NOT stored at the exhibition center?

(A) Diaries
(B) Audio tapes
(C) Photographs
(D) Videos

3. According to the message, which of the following statements is TRUE?

(A) The talk is given by a teacher to her students.

(B) Books and other objects are donated by a private collector.

(C) The writers whose belongings are on exhibition have all passed away.

(D) Permanent exhibits are maintained on both the third and the fourth floors.

Selection 2

4. Which book is the man unable to remember?

(A) *Dream of the Red Chamber*

(B) *Romance of the Three Kingdoms*

(C) *Journey to the West*

(D) *Outlaws of the Marsh*

5. Has the woman ever read *Dream of the Red Chamber*?

(A) She has read the English edition.

(B) She has read the Chinese edition.

(C) She has read both the English and the Chinese editions.

(D) She has read neither the English nor the Chinese edition.

6. Which book does the man want to borrow?

(A) *Dream of the Red Chamber*

(B) *Romance of the Three Kingdoms*

(C) *Journey to the West*

(D) *Outlaws of the Marsh*

Selection 3

7. What is the relationship between Wen Wen and Zhang Lan?

(A) Classmates
(B) Colleagues
(C) Mother and daughter
(D) Teacher and student

8. What has Wen Wen always wanted to buy?

(A) The caricature of *Hua Mulan*

(B) The movie ticket for *Hua Mulan*

(C) The opera ticket for *Hua Mulan*

(D) The DVD of *Hua Mulan*

9. Where did Zhang Lan buy the item Wen Wen was looking for?

   (A) At an opera house

   (B) At a movie theater

   (C) At a bookstore

   (D) At a shop

Selection 4

10. Which country is the leading actress from?

    (A) China

    (B) Thailand

    (C) South Korea

    (D) America

11. What did the woman say about the film?

    (A) It received good reviews from film critics.

    (B) The plot was very dull.

    (C) The acting was not as good as she had expected.

    (D) It was worth watching.

12. According to the conversation, which of the following statements is TRUE?

    (A) The man has not decided if he wants to watch the film.

    (B) The man has decided to invite another person to watch the film with him.

    (C) The man has decided to invite the woman to watch the film again.

    (D) The man has decided not to watch the film.

Selection 5

13. How many people took part in the performance?

    (A) Less than 10   (B) Exactly 20

    (C) More than 20   (D) More than 30

14. Who is most likely the speaker?

    (A) An art director   (B) A leading actress

    (C) A member of the audience (D) A host

15. What is special about the performance?

    (A) The performers do not talk throughout the performance.

    (B) The performance has no music.

    (C) All the performers are deaf-mutes.

    (D) Most of the performers are deaf-mutes.

III. Multiple Choice (Reading)

Note: In this part, you may move back and forth among all the questions.

Directions: You will read several selections in Chinese. Each selection is accompanied by a number of questions in English. For each question, choose the response that is best according to the selection.

Read this e-mail.

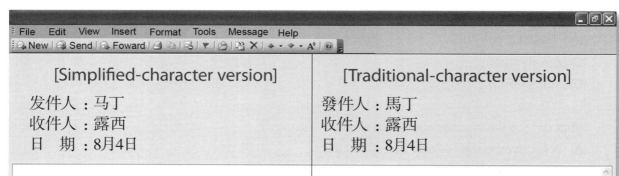

File   Edit   View   Insert   Format   Tools   Message   Help

New   Send   Foward

[Simplified-character version]

发件人：马丁
收件人：露西
日　期：8月4日

露西：
　　你好! 你来中国的机票订好了吗? 订好票的话告诉我一声, 我去机场接你。
　　最近我非常忙, 除了上课之外, 我还在学习中国画。没来中国之前我不太了解中国画, 到这里之后才发现原来它和油画有很大的区别。中国画大多强调表达作者内心的情感, 内容一般以人物、山水、花鸟为主, 画家们通过这些来表达他们的内心世界。中国画是用墨汁来画的, 墨汁的浓淡可以表现出整个画面的气氛。一两句话我也说不清楚, 等你来亲眼看看, 就可以感受到中国画的神奇了。
　　盼望早日见到你! 并祝
　　旅途愉快!
　　　　　　　　　　　马丁
　　　　　　　　　　　8月4日

[Traditional-character version]

發件人：馬丁
收件人：露西
日　期：8月4日

露西：
　　你好! 你來中國的機票訂好了嗎? 訂好票的話告訴我一聲, 我去機場接你。
　　最近我非常忙, 除了上課之外, 我還在學習中國畫。沒來中國之前我不太瞭解中國畫, 到這裏之後才發現原來它和油畫有很大的區別。中國畫大多強調表達作者內心的情感, 内容一般以人物、山水、花鳥爲主, 畫家們通過這些來表達他們的内心世界。中國畫是用墨汁來畫的, 墨汁的濃淡可以表現出整個畫面的氛氛。一兩句話我也說不清楚, 等你來親眼看看, 就可以感受到中國畫的神奇了。
　　盼望早日見到你! 並祝
　　旅途愉快!
　　　　　　　　　　　馬丁
　　　　　　　　　　　8月4日

1. What has Lucy been planning to do lately?

    (A) Learn Chinese

    (B) Learn traditional Chinese painting

    (C) Do research on traditional Chinese painting

    (D) Travel to China

2. According to Martin, why has he been busy?

    (A) He has been attending classes and learning traditional Chinese painting.

    (B) He has been attending classes and doing part-time work.

    (C) He has been learning traditional Chinese painting and working full-time.

    (D) He has been doing research on traditional Chinese painting and working full-time.

3. According to the passage, which of the following corresponds to the characteristics of traditional Chinese painting?

    (A) Traditional Chinese painting uses the same techniques as Western paintings.

    (B) The only three motifs in traditional Chinese paintings are landscapes, flowers, and birds.

    (C) Traditional Chinese painting is done with a brush dipped in oil paints.

    (D) Traditional Chinese painting emphasizes the expression of the painter's emotions and feelings.

Read this information.

[Simplified-character version]	[Traditional-character version]
现在最引人关注的文体之一就是访谈录，而在撰写访谈录方面最有影响的作者之一就是张英。张英用了大量时间和精力对21位著名老作家和年轻作家进行了全面的追踪、访谈，最后结集成一本《文学人生——作家访谈录》。这本访谈录不同于一般记者的采访录，而是体现出采访者与被采访者之间心灵的碰撞。该书思想解放、思维活跃，显示出了一种平等、自由的"对话"精神。这种"对话"为中国文学留下了一大批宝贵的第一手资料。	現在最引人關注的文體之一就是訪談錄，而在撰寫訪談錄方面最有影響的作者之一就是張英。張英用了大量時間和精力對21位著名老作家和年輕作家進行了全面的追蹤、訪談，最後結集成一本《文學人生——作家訪談錄》。這本訪談錄不同於一般記者的採訪錄，而是體現出採訪者與被採訪者之間心靈的碰撞。該書思想解放、思維活躍，顯示出了一種平等、自由的"對話"精神。這種"對話"爲中國文學留下了一大批寶貴的第一手資料。

4. What does the passage introduce?

    (A) A research paper

    (B) A collection of interview records

    (C) An anthology

    (D) A novel

5. What is the focus of the work?

(A) Some moving stories about love

(B) The introduction of a journalist's thoughts

(C) The introduction of a person's life

(D) Notes of conversations with some writers

6. What does "第一手资料（第一手資料）" mean in the passage?

(A) Materials written by hand

(B) Raw materials

(C) Important materials

(D) The first batch of materials

Read this information.

[Simplified-character version]	[Traditional-character version]
中国"全球通"短信文学大赛是由中国移动通信有限公司、《天涯》杂志社和天涯社区联合主办的全国性手机文学比赛。这次大赛已经成功地举办了两届，影响很大，得到了专家、学者及社会各界的充分肯定。本次大赛将向全球华人广泛征集诗歌、散文、小说、幽默笑话、情感类故事、办公室故事、故事接龙等文学作品。 　　大赛开设了短信、上网两种投稿方法。短信费用：1元/条。 　　参赛作品截止日期：2007年9月30日。望广大手机文学爱好者踊跃投稿。	中國"全球通"　　短信文學大賽是由中國移動通信有限公司、《天涯》雜誌社和天涯社區聯合主辦的全國性手機文學比賽。這次大賽已經成功地舉辦了兩屆，影響很大，得到了專家、學者及社會各界的充分肯定。本次大賽將向全球華人廣泛徵集詩歌、散文、小說、幽默笑話、情感類故事、辦公室故事、故事接龍等文學作品。 　　大賽開設了短信、上網兩種投稿方法。短信費用：1元/條。 　　參賽作品截止日期：2007年9月30日。望廣大手機文學愛好者踴躍投稿。

7. This is most likely _____ .

(A) a recruitment notice

(B) a news report

(C) a sales announcement

(D) a competition notice

8. What is the scope of this activity?

(A) It reaches out to the entire district.

(B) It reaches out to the entire city.

(C) It reaches out to the entire country.

(D) It reaches out to the entire world.

9. How can participants submit their work?

(A) Online or by post

(B) By phone call or short message

(C) Online or by short message

(D) By phone call or e-mail

Read this note.

[Simplified-character version]

张华:

　　今天我们课外活动小组的王老师说，要开一个太极拳学习班。你不是一直很想学太极拳吗? 赶快去报名吧! 每个月的学费才100元。每周上两次课，周一和周三的下午3点至4点，正好我们都没有课。周五下午上完课我陪你去王老师办公室报名吧。

　　另外，你让我帮你买的《唐诗三百首》，我已经买到了，报名的时候我给你带去。

　　再联系!

　　　　　　　　　　小林　即日

[Traditional-character version]

張華:

　　今天我們課外活動小組的王老師說，要開一個太極拳學習班。你不是一直很想學太極拳嗎? 趕快去報名吧! 每個月的學費才100元。每週上兩次課，週一和週三的下午3點至4點，正好我們都沒有課。週五下午上完課我陪你去王老師辦公室報名吧。

　　另外，你讓我幫你買的《唐詩三百首》，我已經買到了，報名的時候我給你帶去。

　　再聯繫!

　　　　　　　　　　小林　即日

10. What had Zhang Hua always wanted to learn?

(A) Martial arts

(B) Tang poems

(C) Traditional Chinese music

(D) A foreign language

11. What does Xiao Lin think about the fee of 100 *yuan*?

(A) He finds it very expensive.

(B) He finds it expensive but thinks it is value for money.

(C) He thinks it should be a little cheaper.

(D) He thinks it is not expensive at all.

12. What did Zhang Hua ask Xiao Lin to do?

  (A) Register in an extra-curricular activity

  (B) Register in the Taiji class

  (C) Request Teacher Wang to grant him an absence of leave

  (D) Buy a book

13. What does "即日（即日）"mean?

  (A) A day that is approaching   **(B)** That very day

  (C) These days   **(D)** At once

Read this notice.

[Simplified-character version]

欢迎邮购《汉语世界》！

　　如果您错过了邮局订阅的时间，如果您本来就不喜欢订阅或者不习惯去书摊购买（有的地方不一定能买到），您可以选择邮购的方式。您只须到当地邮局给本刊邮购部一次性汇款120元（全年6期，免邮费），每月的《汉语世界》就会由本刊邮购部直接寄往您的住处。如万一没收到，本刊承诺一定补寄。为免误寄，请一定把您的地址、姓名书写清楚，并注明"购《汉语世界》"。

[Traditional-character version]

歡迎郵購《漢語世界》！

　　如果您錯過了郵局訂閱的時間，如果您本來就不喜歡訂閱或者不習慣去書攤購買（有的地方不一定能買到），您可以選擇郵購的方式。您只須到當地郵局給本刊郵購部一次性匯款120元（全年6期，免郵費），每月的《漢語世界》就會由本刊郵購部直接寄往您的住處。如萬一沒收到，本刊承諾一定補寄。爲免誤寄，請一定把您的地址、姓名書寫清楚，並注明"購《漢語世界》"。

14. According to the notice, which of the following is NOT a way to obtain a copy of 《汉语世界》（《漢語世界》)?

  (A) By subscribing to it at the post office

  (B) By purchasing at a newsstand

  (C) By subscribing through mail order

  (D) By purchasing on the Internet

15. According to the notice, what is《汉语世界》(《漢語世界》)?

(A) A magazine

(B) A weekly newspaper

(C) A music CD

(D) A textbook

16. What should customers do if they do not receive their purchase?

(A) Contact the post office and request for the item to be resent

(B) Contact the mail order department and they will resend the item

(C) Contact the mail order department and they will refund the money

(D) Contact the post office and they will investigate

17. What does "误寄（誤寄）"mean?

(A) The loss of items that were mailed

(B) The damage of items that were mailed

(C) The mistake that occurred in the mailing of items

(D) The second mailing of items

Read this passage.

[Simplified-character version]	[Traditional-character version]
"胎毛"是指孩子刚出生时的头发。按照中国人的习惯，当孩子满月时，要将这种头发全部剃光，以后才能长出好头发。现在独生子女多了，年轻的父母希望为孩子的出世留下永恒的纪念，于是就出现了用胎毛做成的纪念品，例如胎毛画、胎毛笔等。胎毛笔就是将剃下的胎毛收集起来，经过多道工序，加工制成的特殊的"笔"。因为胎毛没有经过修剪，有自然形成的发尖，所以胎毛笔一直被书法家称作"最好用的一种笔"。制作胎毛笔的父母一般都会选价值几百元的材料做笔杆，来与胎毛笔头相配。一个孩子的胎毛一般可以做一两支笔，听说有一家因为孩子出生时就长了一头浓密的头发，他们一下子做了六支笔，除了留给孩子和父母以外，还分别送给爷爷、奶奶、姥姥、姥爷各一支。	"胎毛"是指孩子剛出生時的頭髮。按照中國人的習慣，當孩子滿月時，要將這種頭髮全部剃光，以後才能長出好頭髮。現在獨生子女多了，年輕的父母希望爲孩子的出世留下永恆的紀念，於是就出現了用胎毛做成的紀念品，例如胎毛畫、胎毛筆等。胎毛筆就是將剃下的胎毛收集起來，經過多道工序，加工製成的特殊的"筆"。因爲胎毛沒有經過修剪，有自然形成的髮尖，所以胎毛筆一直被書法家稱作"最好用的一種筆"。製作胎毛筆的父母一般都會選價值幾百元的材料做筆桿，來與胎毛筆頭相配。一個孩子的胎毛一般可以做一兩支筆，聽説有一家因爲孩子出生時就長了一頭濃密的頭髮，他們一下子做了六支筆，除了留給孩子和父母以外，還分別送給爺爺、奶奶、姥姥、姥爺各一支。

18. According to the passage, why do some one-month-old babies have their lanugo hair shaved off?

    (A) In order to make Chinese brushes

    (B) So that their hair may grow back better

    (C) In order to commemorate a special occasion

    (D) So that their parents can have a collection of lanugo hair

19. Approximately how many Chinese brushes can be made using the lanugo hair of a baby?

    (A) 1-2 brushes   (B) 2-3 brushes

    (C) 3-4 brushes   (D) 4-5 brushes

20. According to the passage, why are Chinese brushes made of lanugo hair good?

    (A) They have undergone many processes.

    (B) They are usually accompanied by expensive pen-holders.

    (C) Lanugo hair has natural points.

    (D) Lanugo hair is very thick.

Read this public sign.

[Simplified-character version]

此巷不通

[Traditional-character version]

此巷不通

21. Where would this sign most likely appear?

    (A) In front of an entrance to a building

    (B) At the mouth of a small street

    (C) Beside a lawn

    (D) At the entrance of a subway

22. What is the purpose of this sign?

    (A) To let people know that construction is ongoing

    (B) To let people know that the entrance is closed

    (C) To let people know that no vehicles are allowed in

    (D) To let people know that the street is a dead end

Read this public sign.

[Simplified-character version]

非公莫入

[Traditional-character version]

非公莫入

23. Where would this sign most likely appear?

(A) On a wall

(B) On a window

(C) On a door

(D) On a desk

24. What does "公（公）" in the sign mean?

(A) Business

(B) Public

(C) Male

(D) Workers

Section Two

I.   Free Response (Writing)

Note: In this part, you may NOT move back and forth among questions.

Directions: You will be asked to write in Chinese in a variety of ways. In each case, you will be asked to write for a specific purpose and to a specific person. You should write in as complete and as culturally appropriate a manner as possible, taking into account the purpose and the person described.

1. Story Narration

The four pictures present a story. Imagine you are writing the story to a friend. Narrate a complete story as suggested by the pictures. Give your story a beginning, a middle, and an end.

2. Personal Letter

Imagine you received a letter from a friend. In the letter, he introduces a popular book and suggests you read it. He also hopes you can recommend him some good books. Write a reply in letter format. Introduce him to one good book or a few good books that were published in recent years and that you feel are worth reading. Explain clearly why you recommend them.

3. E-Mail Response

Read this e-mail from a friend and then type a response.

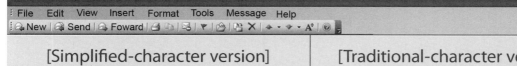

[Simplified-character version]	[Traditional-character version]
发件人: 王龙	發件人: 王龍
主　题: 我最喜欢的文学形象	主　題: 我最喜歡的文學形象

《三国演义》是中国最有名的古典小说之一，我最近一直都在看这本书，书中最让我着迷的人物就数诸葛亮了。诸葛亮有超凡的智慧，经常是事情还没有发生，他就已经知道结果了。其实历史上的诸葛亮并没有这么神奇，但是我还是非常喜欢书中这个人物形象，宁愿相信他的故事都是真实的。你最喜欢的文学作品中的人物形象是谁呢？希望来信聊一聊。	《三國演義》是中國最有名的古典小說之一，我最近一直都在看這本書，書中最讓我着迷的人物就數諸葛亮了。諸葛亮有超凡的智慧，經常是事情還沒有發生，他就已經知道結果了。其實歷史上的諸葛亮並沒有這麼神奇，但是我還是非常喜歡書中這個人物形象，寧願相信他的故事都是真實的。你最喜歡的文學作品中的人物形象是誰呢？希望來信聊一聊。

4. Relay a Telephone Message

Imagine you are sharing an apartment with some Chinese friends. You arrive home one day and listen to a message on the answering machine. The message is for one of your housemates. You will listen twice to the message. Then relay the message, including the important details, by typing an e-mail to your friend.

II. Free Response (Speaking)

Note: In this part, you may NOT move back and forth among questions.

Directions: You will participate in a simulated conversation. Each time it is your turn to speak, you will have 20 seconds to record. You should respond as fully and as appropriately as possible.

1. Conversation

Everyone would have experienced some extent of bewilderment when applying for a university. You chat with your classmate about this.

Directions: You will be asked to speak in Chinese on different topics in the following two questions. In each case, imagine you are making an oral presentation to your class or your family in Chinese. First, you will read and hear the topic for your presentation. You will have 4 minutes to prepare your presentation. Then you will have 2 minutes to record your presentation. Your presentation should be as complete as possible.

2. Cultural Presentation

In your presentation, describe your favorite Chinese song or musical composition. Talk about its basic features and explain why you like it.

3. Event Plan

You are planning to compile your classmates' essays into a book. This book may be organized according to many different themes. In your presentation, first introduce the theme you have selected, then explain the pros and cons of different options. You should also describe in detail your selection criteria for the essays, including the required number of words, how the essay should be submitted, the submission deadline, etc.

UNIT TEN
LESSON 20
Literature and Arts
Chinese Papercutting

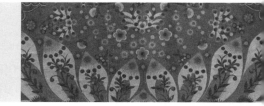

Section One

I. Multiple Choice (Listen to the dialogs)

Note: In this part, you may NOT move back and forth among questions.

Directions: In this part, you will hear several short conversations or parts of conversations followed by four choices, designated (A), (B), (C), and (D). Choose the one that continues or completes the conversation in a logical and culturally appropriate manner. You will have 5 seconds to answer each question.

1.	(A)	(B)	(C)	(D)	5.	(A)	(B)	(C)	(D)
2.	(A)	(B)	(C)	(D)	6.	(A)	(B)	(C)	(D)
3.	(A)	(B)	(C)	(D)	7.	(A)	(B)	(C)	(D)
4.	(A)	(B)	(C)	(D)	8.	(A)	(B)	(C)	(D)

II. Multiple Choice (Listen to the selections)

Note: In this part, you may move back and forth only among the questions associated with the current listening selection.

Directions: In this part, you will listen to several selections in Chinese. For each selection, you will be told whether it will be played once or twice. You may take notes as you listen. After listening to each selection, you will see questions in English. For each question, choose the response that is best according to the selection. You will have 12 seconds to answer each question.

Selection 1

1. Why are the speaker's parents unwilling to let her play football?
   (A) The speaker is a girl.
   (B) The speaker's parents are afraid that her studies may be affected.
   (C) The speaker's parents are afraid that she will get hurt.
   (D) The speaker's health has been deteriorating.

2. Why does the speaker say that she and her friends feel proud?

(A) Many girls do not know how to play football.

(B) They had won the competition.

(C) They work hard for each game.

(D) They are often praised for their skills.

3. What does "对手（對手）" mean?

(A) People who are capable

(B) People who are rivals

(C) People who are standing opposite

(D) People who are participating in a game

Selection 2

4. What did the man sing?

(A) Peking opera

(B) Kunqu opera

(C) Qinqiang opera

(D) Han opera

5. Why has the woman never heard of the opera sung by the man?

(A) The opera is only popular in the Hubei province.

(B) The opera is only popular in Beijing.

(C) The woman did not hear him clearly.

(D) The man has just started to learn the opera.

6. According to the conversation, which of the following statements is TRUE?

(A) Erhuang originates from Peking opera.

(B) Qinqiang opera was derived from other local operas.

(C) Peking opera and Han opera are closely connected with each other.

(D) Peking opera has a longer history than Kunqu opera.

Selection 3

7. Why is the physical examination being rescheduled?

(A) There has been a time conflict between the working hours and the physical examination schedule.

(B) Another hospital has been chosen to perform the physical examination.

(C) Too many people are scheduled to have the physical examination.

(D) Too many people are unable to attend the physical examination.

8. When are female employees scheduled to have their physical examination?

(A) 8:00 am to 11:30 am

(B) 1:00 pm to 5:00 pm

(C) 11:30 am to 1:00 pm

(D) 8:00 am to 5:00 pm

9. What should employees do if they are unable to attend the physical examination at the required time?

(A) Make their own arrangements to have the physical examination done

(B) Call the hospital and request for the physical examination to be conducted the next day

(C) Produce their staff card and have the physical examination performed at noon

(D) Give up the opportunity to undertake the physical examination

Selection 4

10. According to Ms Li, how has Xiao Zhang changed?

(A) She has grown fitter.

(B) She has put on some weight.

(C) She is slimmer.

(D) She looks younger.

11. According to the conversation, what is the reason for Xiao Zhang's change?

(A) She has been working too hard.

(B) She has been taking some medicine.

(C) She has been exercising.

(D) She has been drinking a lot of tea recently.

12. How does Ms Li probably feel about Xiao Zhang's change?

(A) She is understanding.

(B) She is envious.

(C) She does not like it.

(D) She sympathizes with her.

Selection 5

13. Where do young lovers like to frequent?

(A) Bars

(B) Internet bars

(C) Movie bars

(D) Disco bars

14. If a middle-aged man or an elderly man wants to reminisce about the old days, where would he most likely go to?

(A) A bar

(B) An Internet bar

(C) A movie bar

(D) A disco bar

15. According to the message, which of the following statements is TRUE?

(A) The elderly and middle-aged people do not go to Internet bars.

(B) Men like to go to disco bars after work to dance and relax.

(C) The usage of "吧（吧）" in Chinese is much more flexible than that in English.

(D) A disco bar is a place where young people can play snooker.

III. Multiple Choice (Reading)

Note: In this part, you may move back and forth among all the questions.

Directions: You will read several selections in Chinese. Each selection is accompanied by a number of questions in English. For each question, choose the response that is best according to the selection.

Read this passage.

[Simplified-character version]	[Traditional-character version]
2006北京·日本电影周	**2006北京·日本電影週**
"2006北京·日本电影周"将于本月18日至26日在中国电影资料馆举办。此次电影周将放映不同时期、不同风格的11部优秀日本电影。包括黑泽明的经典之作《椿三十郎》、山田洋次的《寅次郎的故事——紫阳花之恋》、恐怖片《妖怪大战争》、数字版动画片《银河铁道之夜》、故事片《春雪》以及日本11月3日刚上映的社会情感片《信》。欢迎广大电影爱好者前来观看。订票超过5个场次的观众将得到精美电影海报一张！	"2006北京·日本電影週"將於本月18日至26日在中國電影資料館舉辦。此次電影週將放映不同時期、不同風格的11部優秀日本電影。包括黑澤明的經典之作《椿三十郎》、山田洋次的《寅次郎的故事——紫陽花之戀》、恐怖片《妖怪大戰爭》、數字版動畫片《銀河鐵道之夜》、故事片《春雪》以及日本11月3日剛上映的社會情感片《信》。歡迎廣大電影愛好者前來觀看。訂票超過5個場次的觀眾將得到精美電影海報一張！
订票热线: 010–58804590	訂票熱線: 010–58804590
中国电影资料馆 2006年11月1日	中國電影資料館 2006年11月1日

1. What is TRUE about the "Japanese Film Week"?

(A) It lasted for seven days.

(B) All films shown in the week were filmed by famous directors.

(C) Both old and new films were shown during the week.

(D) All the films shown in the week had the same theme.

2. How could one get a film poster?
    (A) Filmgoers who purchased tickets by phone were entitled to one poster.
    (B) Filmgoers who had watched more than five films were entitled to one poster.
    (C) Filmgoers who were the first to purchase the tickets of each film were entitled to one poster.
    (D) Filmgoers who had watched both last year and this year's films were entitled to one poster.

Read this passage.

[Simplified-character version]	[Traditional-character version]
在很久以前，楚国有一位著名的音乐大师叫俞伯牙，他因弹得一手好琴而远近闻名，大家都说没有人比他弹得更好。这位琴师有一个特别要好的朋友，叫钟子期。钟子期之所以能成为俞伯牙的好朋友，并不是因为他也能弹一手好琴，而是在于他特别能理解俞伯牙琴声中的含义。他们都特别喜欢一支叫《高山流水》的乐曲。后来钟子期病死了，俞伯牙觉得失去了知音，非常悲痛，就在钟子期的墓前弹奏了那首《高山流水》之后，把琴摔坏了，并且从此不再弹琴。	在很久以前，楚國有一位著名的音樂大師叫俞伯牙，他因彈得一手好琴而遠近聞名，大家都説沒有人比他彈得更好。這位琴師有一個特別要好的朋友，叫鐘子期。鐘子期之所以能成爲俞伯牙的好朋友，並不是因爲他也能彈一手好琴，而是在於他特別能理解俞伯牙琴聲中的含義。他們都特別喜歡一支叫《高山流水》的樂曲。後來鐘子期病死了，俞伯牙覺得失去了知音，非常悲痛，就在鐘子期的墓前彈奏了那首《高山流水》之後，把琴摔壞了，並且從此不再彈琴。

3. Why is Yu Boya said to be "远近闻名（遠近聞名）"?
    (A) Many people have heard of him.
    (B) The music he produces is loud and clear and can be heard far away.
    (C) Many people have heard him playing the *qin*.
    (D) He has a lot of friends.

4. How did Zhong Ziqi become Yu Boya's good friend?
    (A) He can play the *qin* better than Yu Boya.
    (B) He can play the *qin* as well as Yu Boya.
    (C) He can understand Yu Boya's music.
    (D) He writes all the music that is played by Yu Boya.

5. Why did Yu Boya stop playing the *qin*?

(A) The *qin* was damaged.

(B) He had lost his bosom friend.

(C) He was seriously ill.

(D) He had lost his musical skills.

Read this letter.

[Simplified-character version]

王莹：

你在上海的实习顺利吗？很忙吧？

你知道今天谁来咱们学校做讲座了吗？是著名的现代文学教授张明，他的讲座风趣、幽默，学校的大礼堂里挤得满满的，连过道都站满了人，大家听得都特别认真。为了听这次讲座，昨天我还特意翻了翻他的那本《中国现代文学史》，所以今天听讲座的时候感觉思路特别清晰。真可惜你错过了这次好机会，不过没关系，我帮你录了音，你回来后可以听。

你可以帮我买这位先生的书吗？我跑遍了这边的书店也没有买到，拜托你帮我到上海的书店看看，谢谢！

什么时候回来？提前通知我一声，我好去车站接你！

祝

心情愉快！

美凤

[Traditional-character version]

王瑩：

你在上海的實習順利嗎？很忙吧？

你知道今天誰來咱們學校做講座了嗎？是著名的現代文學教授張明，他的講座風趣、幽默，學校的大禮堂裏擠得滿滿的，連過道都站滿了人，大家聽得都特別認真。爲了聽這次講座，昨天我還特意翻了翻他的那本《中國現代文學史》，所以今天聽講座的時候感覺思路特別清晰。真可惜你錯過了這次好機會，不過沒關係，我幫你錄了音，你回來後可以聽。

你可以幫我買這位先生的書嗎？我跑遍了這邊的書店也沒有買到，拜托你幫我到上海的書店看看，謝謝！

什麼時候回來？提前通知我一聲，我好去車站接你！

祝

心情愉快！

美鳳

6. How did the lecture mentioned in the letter go?

(A) There was only a small audience but the atmosphere was good.

(B) There was a large audience and the lecture was wonderful.

(C) There was only a small audience but the lecture was interesting.

(D) There was a large audience but the lecture was mediocre.

7. According to Mei Feng, how did she manage to keep a clear mind during the lecture?

(A) The lecture was wonderful.

(B) She listened very carefully.

(C) The lecture topic was one of her subjects in school.

(D) She did some preparation for the lecture.

8. Why did Wang Ying NOT go for the lecture?

(A) She had to go for a meeting.

(B) She had to go for an internship.

(C) She had to go buy some books.

(D) She had to attend some classes.

9. Why does Mei Feng ask Wang Ying to buy some books for her?

(A) She does not have time to buy the books.

(B) She has not been able to locate the books.

(C) She does not know where the bookstore is.

(D) She is not feeling well.

Read this story.

[Simplified-character version]	[Traditional-character version]
过去贵州这个地方没有驴,于是,有人用船运来了一头驴,运来后却发现没有什么用处,就把驴放到山脚下。一只老虎看到驴,以为这个大家伙一定很厉害,就躲在树林里偷偷地观察。后来它悄悄走出来,小心翼翼地接近驴。这时,驴大叫了一声,老虎大吃一惊,马上远远地躲开,以为驴要吃自己,所以非常恐惧。然而,驴却再也没有什么别的动作了,老虎就又悄悄地接近驴。经过反复观察,老虎觉得驴并没有什么特殊本领。于是,它就大吼一声扑了过去,把驴吃掉了。	過去貴州這個地方沒有驢,於是,有人用船運來了一頭驢,運來後卻發現沒有什麼用處,就把驢放到山腳下。一隻老虎看到驢,以爲這個大傢伙一定很屬害,就躲在樹林裏偷偷地觀察。後來牠悄悄走出來,小心翼翼地接近驢。這時,驢大叫了一聲,老虎大吃一驚,馬上遠遠地躲開,以爲驢要吃自己,所以非常恐懼。然而,驢卻再也沒有什麼別的動作了,老虎就又悄悄地接近驢。經過反復觀察,老虎覺得驢並沒有什麼特殊本領。於是,牠就大吼一聲撲了過去,把驢吃掉了。

10. Why were the donkeys transported to Guizhou?

(A) The people in Guizhou thought donkeys were lovely creatures.

(B) There were no donkeys in Guizhou initially.

(C) There was a need for donkeys in Guizhou.

(D) The people in Guizhou wanted to rear donkeys.

11. According to the story, which of the following statements is TRUE?

    (A) The tiger was afraid of the donkey at the beginning.

    (B) The tiger thought the donkey was lovely.

    (C) The tiger hoped to befriend the donkey.

    (D) The tiger was never afraid of the donkey.

12. Why did the tiger approach the donkey at times and avoid it at other times?

    (A) It was playing with the donkey.

    (B) It was testing the donkey.

    (C) It was contemplating on what it should do.

    (D) It was trying to frighten the donkey.

13. What traits does the donkey in the story possess?

    (A) It is foolish to challenge the tiger.

    (B) It is big but useless.

    (C) It is disobedient and noisy.

    (D) It is big and talented.

Read this passage.

[Simplified-character version]	[Traditional-character version]
最近南京的十多位普通工人、教师和农民工，通过江苏唱片有限公司的录音室制作了个人录音带。据介绍，录音室与卡拉OK厅最大的区别是，录音室能对声音进行加工，帮你弥补各种不足。比如有的人唱不了高音，可以通过"提音"来完成；有的人嗓子哑了，通过处理可以使声音变得圆润好听；即使你从来唱不了一首完整的歌，经过加工也能把你零散的歌声变成完整的一首歌。该公司的经理说："你只要把音唱准，别的事都交给我们来做。"制作公司还会为你的录音带做出漂亮的彩封，和市场上卖的录音带几乎一模一样。不过这项服务的费用不算便宜，需要两三千块钱。现在北京、山东等几个地方也开始出现经营这种业务的公司了。	最近南京的十多位普通工人、教師和農民工，通過江蘇唱片有限公司的錄音室製作了個人錄音帶。據介紹，錄音室與卡拉OK廳最大的區別是，錄音室能對聲音進行加工，幫你彌補各種不足。比如有的人唱不了高音，可以通過"提音"來完成；有的人嗓子啞了，通過處理可以使聲音變得圓潤好聽；即使你從來唱不了一首完整的歌，經過加工也能把你零散的歌聲變成完整的一首歌。該公司的經理說："你只要把音唱準，別的事都交給我們來做。"製作公司還會爲你的錄音帶做出漂亮的彩封，和市場上賣的錄音帶幾乎一模一樣。不過這項服務的費用不算便宜，需要兩三千塊錢。現在北京、山東等幾個地方也開始出現經營這種業務的公司了。

14. What is the main difference between a recording studio and a karaoke hall?
    (A) A recording studio charges a lower fee than a karaoke hall.
    (B) A recording studio is open to everyone.
    (C) A recording studio can preserve a person's unique vocal style.
    (D) A recording studio allows manipulation of the sound quality.

15. What problem cannot be solved in a recording studio?
    (A) One's voice is hoarse and not melodious.
    (B) One's vocal range is limited and cannot reach a high pitch.
    (C) One has no pitch sense and cannot hold a tune.
    (D) One cannot remember the lyrics and cannot complete a song.

16. What does "彩封（彩封）" mean?
    (A) Colorful envelopes
    (B) Colorful packaging
    (C) Colorful seals
    (D) Colorful illustrations

17. What is the current situation for making personal audio tapes?
    (A) It is popular nationwide.
    (B) It is only popular in South China.
    (C) It is only popular in Nanjing.
    (D) It is not very popular nationwide.

Read this passage.

[Simplified-character version]	[Traditional-character version]
小时候，我家有棵果树一直不结果。奶奶查了很多书，又和邻居们讨论了很久，无论是多浇水，还是多施肥，效果都不好。后来，她去请教加州的一位农业专家，得到一个不可思议的建议：用棍棒击打果树的根基，以此来刺激它的根系。那时，每当看见奶奶用棍棒"教训"不结果的果树时，我们都会不由得发笑。我们也担心邻居们看到时，会认为奶奶已经老糊涂了，可是奶奶并不在乎。到了第二年，我们惊讶地发现，果树奇迹般地开花结果了。长大后，我曾经历了一段非常艰难的日子。我给奶奶打电话，聊起那段经历时，奶奶提醒我说，恶劣的环境就像当年击打果树的棍棒一样，不停地刺激着我，也正因为这样，我才会变得成熟，收获也才会更大。	小時候，我家有棵果樹一直不結果。奶奶查了很多書，又和鄰居們討論了很久，無論是多澆水，還是多施肥，效果都不好。後來，她去請教加州的一位農業專家，得到一個不可思議的建議：用棍棒擊打果樹的根基，以此來刺激它的根系。那時，每當看見奶奶用棍棒"教訓"不結果的果樹時，我們都會不由得發笑。我們也擔心鄰居們看到時，會認爲奶奶已經老糊塗了，可是奶奶並不在乎。到了第二年，我們驚訝地發現，果樹奇蹟般地開花結果了。長大後，我曾經歷了一段非常艱難的日子。我給奶奶打電話，聊起那段經歷時，奶奶提醒我說，惡劣的環境就像當年擊打果樹的棍棒一樣，不停地刺激著我，也正因爲這樣，我才會變得成熟，收獲也才會更大。

18. How did the grandmother discover the way to cause the fruit tree to bear fruits?

   (A) She discussed with the neighbors.

   (B) She consulted an expert.

   (C) She discussed with her children.

   (D) She referred to some professional books.

19. What does "不可思议（不可思議）" mean in the passage?

   (A) Illogical

   (B) Impractical

   (C) Inconceivable

   (D) Unconventional

20. At the beginning, what did the children think of their grandmother's method?

   (A) They thought she was confused.

   (B) They thought her method was great.

   (C) They thought she was very professional.

   (D) They thought her method was very funny.

21. What does the story illustrate?

(A) We should always persevere to achieve our goals.

(B) Adversities can make one a better person.

(C) We should continually seek unconventional ways of doing things.

(D) Adversities can help bring about monetary gains.

Read this public sign.

[Simplified-character version]

假一赔十

[Traditional-character version]

假一賠十

22. Where would this sign most likely appear?

(A) In a consumer rights organization

(B) In a canteen

(C) In a store

(D) On a billboard

23. What is the purpose of this sign?

(A) To remind customers not to buy fake products

(B) To warn the sellers not to sell fake products

(C) To publicize that there are no fake products

(D) To protest against fake products

Read this public sign.

[Simplified-character version]

挂号请排队

[Traditional-character version]

掛號請排隊

24. Where would this sign most likely appear?

(A) At a bus station

(B) In a canteen

(C) In a hospital

(D) In a park

25. Which of the following statements about this sign is TRUE?

(A) It says that people should queue if they wish to register.

(B) It says that it is important to queue in an orderly manner.

(C) It says that people should wait patiently for their turn.

(D) It says that everyone should register before joining the queue.

Section Two

I.   Free Response (Writing)

Note: In this part, you may NOT move back and forth among questions.

Directions: You will be asked to write in Chinese in a variety of ways. In each case, you will be asked to write for a specific purpose and to a specific person. You should write in as complete and as culturally appropriate a manner as possible, taking into account the purpose and the person described.

1. Story Narration

The four pictures present a story. Imagine you are writing the story to a friend. Narrate a complete story as suggested by the pictures. Give your story a beginning, a middle, and an end.

2. Personal Letter

Imagine you received a letter from a pen pal. In the letter, he tells you about his passion for painting and how it helps him forget the worries of daily life. Write a reply in letter format. In your letter, tell him what you think about learning a particular art skill and how such a study may influence one's well-being.

3. E-Mail Response

Read this e-mail from a friend and then type a response.

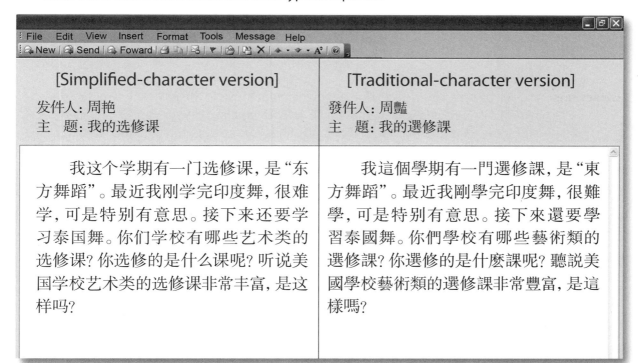

File　Edit　View　Insert　Format　Tools　Message　Help

New　Send　Foward

[Simplified-character version]	[Traditional-character version]
发件人: 周艳 主　题: 我的选修课	發件人: 周豔 主　題: 我的選修課
我这个学期有一门选修课, 是 "东方舞蹈"。最近我刚学完印度舞, 很难学, 可是特别有意思。接下来还要学习泰国舞。你们学校有哪些艺术类的选修课? 你选修的是什么课呢? 听说美国学校艺术类的选修课非常丰富, 是这样吗?	我這個學期有一門選修課, 是 "東方舞蹈"。最近我剛學完印度舞, 很難學, 可是特別有意思。接下來還要學習泰國舞。你們學校有哪些藝術類的選修課? 你選修的是什麼課呢? 聽説美國學校藝術類的選修課非常豐富, 是這樣嗎?

4. Relay a Telephone Message

Imagine you are sharing an apartment with some Chinese friends. You arrive home one day and listen to a message on the answering machine. The message is for one of your housemates. You will listen twice to the message. Then relay the message, including the important details, by typing an e-mail to your friend.

II. Free Response (Speaking)

Note: In this part, you may NOT move back and forth among questions.

Directions: You will participate in a simulated conversation. Each time it is your turn to speak, you will have 20 seconds to record. You should respond as fully and as appropriately as possible.

1. Conversation

Your school has recently organized a performance to celebrate a festival. You chat with your chinese cyber friend about it.

Directions: You will be asked to speak in Chinese on different topics in the following two questions. In each case, imagine you are making an oral presentation to your class or your family in Chinese. First, you will read and hear the topic for your presentation. You will have 4 minutes to prepare your presentation. Then you will have 2 minutes to record your presentation. Your presentation should be as complete as possible.

2. Cultural Presentation

Give an introduction of ONE Chinese artform (such as papercutting, Peking opera, Chinese painting) that you admire or know about. In your presentation, describe the basic features of this artform and explain why you like it.

3. Event Plan

Your uncle's child will be coming to the United States from Hong Kong to live with you soon. This is the first time he is traveling to the United States. Your uncle hopes that you can help him with his English. You are to make two plans to help your cousin learn English and then allow him to select the one he is comfortable with. In your presentation, elaborate on what you intend to do and why, and include the advantages and disadvantages of each plan.

Answer Sheets

(for Section One)

UNIT SIX
LESSON 11
Man and Nature
When a Tsunami Hits

Answer Sheets

Name: _____

Section One

I. Multiple Choice (Listen to the dialogs)
Circle your answers.

1.	(A)	(B)	(C)	(D)	5.	(A)	(B)	(C)	(D)
2.	(A)	(B)	(C)	(D)	6.	(A)	(B)	(C)	(D)
3.	(A)	(B)	(C)	(D)	7.	(A)	(B)	(C)	(D)
4.	(A)	(B)	(C)	(D)	8.	(A)	(B)	(C)	(D)

II. Multiple Choice (Listen to the selections)
Write your answers (A, B, C, or D) in the blanks.

1. (   )   2. (   )   3. (   )   4. (   )   5. (   )

6. (   )   7. (   )   8. (   )   9. (   )   10. (   )

11. (   )   12. (   )   13. (   )   14. (   )   15. (   )

III. Multiple Choice (Reading)
Write your answers (A, B, C, or D) in the blanks.

1. (   )   2. (   )   3. (   )   4. (   )   5. (   )

6. (   )   7. (   )   8. (   )   9. (   )   10. (   )

11. (   )   12. (   )   13. (   )   14. (   )   15. (   )

16. (   )   17. (   )   18. (   )   19. (   )   20. (   )

21. (   )   22. (   )   23. (   )   24. (   )   25. (   )

UNIT SIX
LESSON 12
Man and Nature
Where Will We Live Tomorrow

Answer Sheets

Name: _____

Section One

I. Multiple Choice (Listen to the dialogs)
Circle your answers.

1.	(A)	(B)	(C)	(D)	5.	(A)	(B)	(C)	(D)
2.	(A)	(B)	(C)	(D)	6.	(A)	(B)	(C)	(D)
3.	(A)	(B)	(C)	(D)	7.	(A)	(B)	(C)	(D)
4.	(A)	(B)	(C)	(D)	8.	(A)	(B)	(C)	(D)

II. Multiple Choice (Listen to the selections)
Write your answers (A, B, C, or D) in the blanks.

1. (   )　　2. (   )　　3. (   )　　4. (   )　　5. (   )

6. (   )　　7. (   )　　8. (   )　　9. (   )　　10. (   )

11. (   )　　12. (   )　　13. (   )　　14. (   )　　15. (   )

III. Multiple Choice (Reading)
Write your answers (A, B, C, or D) in the blanks.

1. (   )　　2. (   )　　3. (   )　　4. (   )　　5. (   )

6. (   )　　7. (   )　　8. (   )　　9. (   )　　10. (   )

11. (   )　　12. (   )　　13. (   )　　14. (   )　　15. (   )

16. (   )　　17. (   )　　18. (   )　　19. (   )　　20. (   )

21. (   )　　22. (   )　　23. (   )　　24. (   )　　25. (   )

UNIT SEVEN People and Society
LESSON 13 The Hospitable Southwest

Answer Sheets

Name: _____

Section One

I. Multiple Choice (Listen to the dialogs)
Circle your answers.

1.	(A)	(B)	(C)	(D)	5.	(A)	(B)	(C)	(D)
2.	(A)	(B)	(C)	(D)	6.	(A)	(B)	(C)	(D)
3.	(A)	(B)	(C)	(D)	7.	(A)	(B)	(C)	(D)
4.	(A)	(B)	(C)	(D)	8.	(A)	(B)	(C)	(D)

II. Multiple Choice (Listen to the selections)
Write your answers (A, B, C, or D) in the blanks.

1. (　) 　2. (　) 　3. (　) 　4. (　) 　5. (　)

6. (　) 　7. (　) 　8. (　) 　9. (　) 　10. (　)

11. (　) 　12. (　) 　13. (　) 　14. (　) 　15. (　)

III. Multiple Choice (Reading)
Write your answers (A, B, C, or D) in the blanks.

1. (　) 　2. (　) 　3. (　) 　4. (　) 　5. (　)

6. (　) 　7. (　) 　8. (　) 　9. (　) 　10. (　)

11. (　) 　12. (　) 　13. (　) 　14. (　) 　15. (　)

16. (　) 　17. (　) 　18. (　) 　19. (　) 　20. (　)

21. (　) 　22. (　) 　23. (　) 　24. (　) 　25. (　)

UNIT SEVEN People and Society
LESSON 14 Moving into a Modern Apartment

Answer Sheets

Name: _____

Section One

I. Multiple Choice (Listen to the dialogs)
Circle your answers.

1.	(A)	(B)	(C)	(D)	5.	(A)	(B)	(C)	(D)
2.	(A)	(B)	(C)	(D)	6.	(A)	(B)	(C)	(D)
3.	(A)	(B)	(C)	(D)	7.	(A)	(B)	(C)	(D)
4.	(A)	(B)	(C)	(D)	8.	(A)	(B)	(C)	(D)

II. Multiple Choice (Listen to the selections)
Write your answers (A, B, C, or D) in the blanks.

1. (   ) 2. (   ) 3. (   ) 4. (   ) 5. (   )
6. (   ) 7. (   ) 8. (   ) 9. (   ) 10. (   )
11. (   ) 12. (   ) 13. (   ) 14. (   ) 15. (   )
16. (   )

III. Multiple Choice (Reading)
Write your answers (A, B, C, or D) in the blanks.

1. (   ) 2. (   ) 3. (   ) 4. (   ) 5. (   )
6. (   ) 7. (   ) 8. (   ) 9. (   ) 10. (   )
11. (   ) 12. (   ) 13. (   ) 14. (   ) 15. (   )
16. (   ) 17. (   ) 18. (   ) 19. (   ) 20. (   )
21. (   ) 22. (   ) 23. (   ) 24. (   ) 25. (   )

UNIT SIX
LESSON 15
Chinese Language and Characters
Characters Relating to Animals

Answer Sheets

Name: _____

Section One

I. Multiple Choice (Listen to the dialogs)
Circle your answers.

1.	(A)	(B)	(C)	(D)	5.	(A)	(B)	(C)	(D)
2.	(A)	(B)	(C)	(D)	6.	(A)	(B)	(C)	(D)
3.	(A)	(B)	(C)	(D)	7.	(A)	(B)	(C)	(D)
4.	(A)	(B)	(C)	(D)	8.	(A)	(B)	(C)	(D)

II. Multiple Choice (Listen to the selections)
Write your answers (A, B, C, or D) in the blanks.

1. (   )   2. (   )   3. (   )   4. (   )   5. (   )

6. (   )   7. (   )   8. (   )   9. (   )   10. (   )

11. (   )   12. (   )   13. (   )   14. (   )

III. Multiple Choice (Reading)
Write your answers (A, B, C, or D) in the blanks.

1. (   )   2. (   )   3. (   )   4. (   )   5. (   )

6. (   )   7. (   )   8. (   )   9. (   )   10. (   )

11. (   )   12. (   )   13. (   )   14. (   )   15. (   )

16. (   )   17. (   )   18. (   )   19. (   )   20. (   )

21. (   )   22. (   )   23. (   )   24. (   )   25. (   )

UNIT EIGHT Chinese Language and Characters
LESSON 16 "Prosperity Has Arrived!"

Answer Sheets

Name: _____

Section One

I. Multiple Choice (Listen to the dialogs)
Circle your answers.

1.	(A)	(B)	(C)	(D)	5.	(A)	(B)	(C)	(D)
2.	(A)	(B)	(C)	(D)	6.	(A)	(B)	(C)	(D)
3.	(A)	(B)	(C)	(D)	7.	(A)	(B)	(C)	(D)
4.	(A)	(B)	(C)	(D)	8.	(A)	(B)	(C)	(D)

II. Multiple Choice (Listen to the selections)
Write your answers (A, B, C, or D) in the blanks.

1. (   )   2. (   )   3. (   )   4. (   )   5. (   )

6. (   )   7. (   )   8. (   )   9. (   )   10. (   )

11. (   )   12. (   )   13. (   )   14. (   )   15. (   )

III. Multiple Choice (Reading)
Write your answers (A, B, C, or D) in the blanks.

1. (   )   2. (   )   3. (   )   4. (   )   5. (   )

6. (   )   7. (   )   8. (   )   9. (   )   10. (   )

11. (   )   12. (   )   13. (   )   14. (   )   15. (   )

16. (   )   17. (   )   18. (   )   19. (   )   20. (   )

21. (   )   22. (   )   23. (   )   24. (   )   25. (   )

UNIT NINE
LESSON 17
Famous People and History
Who Was Confucius?

Answer Sheets

Name: _____

Section One

I. Multiple Choice (Listen to the dialogs)
Circle your answers.

1.	(A)	(B)	(C)	(D)	5.	(A)	(B)	(C)	(D)
2.	(A)	(B)	(C)	(D)	6.	(A)	(B)	(C)	(D)
3.	(A)	(B)	(C)	(D)	7.	(A)	(B)	(C)	(D)
4.	(A)	(B)	(C)	(D)	8.	(A)	(B)	(C)	(D)

II. Multiple Choice (Listen to the selections)
Write your answers (A, B, C, or D) in the blanks.

1. (　　)　　2. (　　)　　3. (　　)　　4. (　　)　　5. (　　)

6. (　　)　　7. (　　)　　8. (　　)　　9. (　　)　　10. (　　)

11. (　　)　　12. (　　)　　13. (　　)　　14. (　　)　　15. (　　)

III. Multiple Choice (Reading)
Write your answers (A, B, C, or D) in the blanks.

1. (　　)　　2. (　　)　　3. (　　)　　4. (　　)　　5. (　　)

6. (　　)　　7. (　　)　　8. (　　)　　9. (　　)　　10. (　　)

11. (　　)　　12. (　　)　　13. (　　)　　14. (　　)　　15. (　　)

16. (　　)　　17. (　　)　　18. (　　)　　19. (　　)　　20. (　　)

21. (　　)　　22. (　　)　　23. (　　)　　24. (　　)　　25. (　　)

UNIT NINE
Famous People and History
LESSON 18 China Highlights

Answer Sheets

Name: _____

Section One

I. Multiple Choice (Listen to the dialogs)
Circle your answers.

1.	(A)	(B)	(C)	(D)	5.	(A)	(B)	(C)	(D)
2.	(A)	(B)	(C)	(D)	6.	(A)	(B)	(C)	(D)
3.	(A)	(B)	(C)	(D)	7.	(A)	(B)	(C)	(D)
4.	(A)	(B)	(C)	(D)	8.	(A)	(B)	(C)	(D)

II. Multiple Choice (Listen to the selections)
Write your answers (A, B, C, or D) in the blanks.

1. (   )   2. (   )   3. (   )   4. (   )   5. (   )

6. (   )   7. (   )   8. (   )   9. (   )   10. (   )

11. (   )   12. (   )   13. (   )   14. (   )   15. (   )

III. Multiple Choice (Reading)
Write your answers (A, B, C, or D) in the blanks.

1. (   )   2. (   )   3. (   )   4. (   )   5. (   )

6. (   )   7. (   )   8. (   )   9. (   )   10. (   )

11. (   )   12. (   )   13. (   )   14. (   )   15. (   )

16. (   )   17. (   )   18. (   )   19. (   )   20. (   )

21. (   )   22. (   )   23. (   )   24. (   )   25. (   )

UNIT TEN
LESSON 19 Literature and Arts
"To Borrow Arrows with Thatched Boats"

Answer Sheets

Name: _____

Section One

I. Multiple Choice (Listen to the dialogs)
Circle your answers.

1.	(A)	(B)	(C)	(D)	5.	(A)	(B)	(C)	(D)
2.	(A)	(B)	(C)	(D)	6.	(A)	(B)	(C)	(D)
3.	(A)	(B)	(C)	(D)	7.	(A)	(B)	(C)	(D)
4.	(A)	(B)	(C)	(D)	8.	(A)	(B)	(C)	(D)

II. Multiple Choice (Listen to the selections)
Write your answers (A, B, C, or D) in the blanks.

1. (   )   2. (   )   3. (   )   4. (   )   5. (   )

6. (   )   7. (   )   8. (   )   9. (   )   10. (   )

11. (   )   12. (   )   13. (   )   14. (   )   15. (   )

III. Multiple Choice (Reading)
Write your answers (A, B, C, or D) in the blanks.

1. (   )   2. (   )   3. (   )   4. (   )   5. (   )

6. (   )   7. (   )   8. (   )   9. (   )   10. (   )

11. (   )   12. (   )   13. (   )   14. (   )   15. (   )

16. (   )   17. (   )   18. (   )   19. (   )   20. (   )

21. (   )   22. (   )   23. (   )   24. (   )

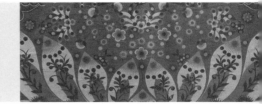

UNIT TEN
LESSON 20 Literature and Arts
Chinese Papercutting

Answer Sheets

Name: _____

Section One

I. Multiple Choice (Listen to the dialogs)
Circle your answers.

1.	(A)	(B)	(C)	(D)	5.	(A)	(B)	(C)	(D)
2.	(A)	(B)	(C)	(D)	6.	(A)	(B)	(C)	(D)
3.	(A)	(B)	(C)	(D)	7.	(A)	(B)	(C)	(D)
4.	(A)	(B)	(C)	(D)	8.	(A)	(B)	(C)	(D)

II. Multiple Choice (Listen to the selections)
Write your answers (A, B, C, or D) in the blanks.

1. ( )　　2. ( )　　3. ( )　　4. ( )　　5. ( )

6. ( )　　7. ( )　　8. ( )　　9. ( )　　10. ( )

11. ( )　　12. ( )　　13. ( )　　14. ( )　　15. ( )

III. Multiple Choice (Reading)
Write your answers (A, B, C, or D) in the blanks.

1. ( )　　2. ( )　　3. ( )　　4. ( )　　5. ( )

6. ( )　　7. ( )　　8. ( )　　9. ( )　　10. ( )

11. ( )　　12. ( )　　13. ( )　　14. ( )　　15. ( )

16. ( )　　17. ( )　　18. ( )　　19. ( )　　20. ( )

21. ( )　　22. ( )　　23. ( )　　24. ( )　　25. ( )